S0-DGK-318

MIDP 2.0 Style Guide

for the

Java™ 2 Platform, Micro Edition

The Java™ Series

Lisa Friendly, Series Editor
Tim Lindholm, Technical Editor
Ken Arnold, Technical Editor of The Jini™ Technology Series
Jim Inscore, Technical Editor of The Java™ Series, Enterprise Edition   **http://www.javaseries.com**

Eric Armstrong, Stephanie Bodoff, Debbie Carson, Maydene Fisher, Dale Green, Kim Haase
The Java™ Web Services Tutorial

Ken Arnold, James Gosling, David Holmes
The Java™ Programming Language, Third Edition

Cindy Bloch, Annette Wagner
MIDP 2.0 Style Guide

Joshua Bloch
Effective Java™ Programming Language Guide

Mary Campione, Kathy Walrath, Alison Huml
The Java™ Tutorial, Third Edition: A Short Course on the Basics

Mary Campione, Kathy Walrath, Alison Huml,Tutorial Team
The Java™ Tutorial Continued: The Rest of the JDK™

Patrick Chan
The Java™ Developers Almanac 1.4, Volume 1

Patrick Chan
The Java™ Developers Almanac 1.4, Volume 2

Patrick Chan, Rosanna Lee
The Java™ Class Libraries, Second Edition, Volume 2: java.applet, java.awt, java.beans

Patrick Chan, Rosanna Lee, Doug Kramer
The Java™ Class Libraries, Second Edition, Volume 1: java.io, java.lang, java.math, java.net, java.text, java.util

Patrick Chan, Rosanna Lee, Doug Kramer
The Java™ Class Libraries, Second Edition, Volume 1: Supplement for the Java™ 2 Platform, Standard Edition, v1.2

Kirk Chen, Li Gong
Programming Open Service Gateways with Java™ Embedded Server

Zhiqun Chen
Java Card™ Technology for Smart Cards: Architecture and Programmer's Guide

Maydene Fisher, Jon Ellis, Jonathan Bruce
JDBC™ API Tutorial and Reference, Third Edition

Li Gong, Gary Ellison, Mary Dageforde
Inside Java™ 2 Platform Security, Second Edition: Architecture, API Design, and Implementation

James Gosling, Bill Joy, Guy Steele, Gilad Bracha
The Java™ Language Specification, Second Edition

Doug Lea
Concurrent Programming in Java™, Second Edition: Design Principles and Patterns

Rosanna Lee, Scott Seligman
JNDI API Tutorial and Reference: Building Directory-Enabled Java™ Applications

Sheng Liang
The Java™ Native Interface: Programmer's Guide and Specification

Tim Lindholm, Frank Yellin
The Java™ Virtual Machine Specification, Second Edition

Roger Riggs, Antero Taivalsaari, Jim Van Peursem, Jyri Huopaniemi, Mark Patel, Aleksi Uotila
Programming Wireless Devices with the Java™ 2 Platform, Micro Edition, Second Edition

Henry Sowizral, Kevin Rushforth, Michael Deering
The Java 3D™ API Specification, Second Edition

Sun Microsystems, Inc.
Java™ Look and Feel Design Guidelines: Advanced Topics

Kathy Walrath, Mary Campione
The JFC Swing Tutorial: A Guide to Constructing GUIs

Seth White, Maydene Fisher, Rick Cattell, Graham Hamilton, Mark Hapner
JDBC™ API Tutorial and Reference, Second Edition: Universal Data Access for the Java™ 2 Platform

Steve Wilson, Jeff Kesselman
Java™ Platform Performance: Strategies and Tactics

The Jini™ Technology Series

Eric Freeman, Susanne Hupfer, Ken Arnold
JavaSpaces™ Principles, Patterns, and Practice

The Java™ Series, Enterprise Edition

Stephanie Bodoff, Dale Green, Kim Haase, Eric Jendrock, Monica Pawlan, Beth Stearns
The J2EE™ Tutorial

Rick Cattell, Jim Inscore, Enterprise Partners
J2EE™ Technology in Practice: Building Business Applications with the Java™ 2 Platform, Enterprise Edition

Mark Hapner, Rich Burridge, Rahul Sharma, Joseph Fialli, Kim Haase
Java™ Message Service API Tutorial and Reference: Messaging for the J2EE™ Platform

Inderjeet Singh, Beth Stearns, Mark Johnson, Enterprise Team
Designing Enterprise Applications with the Java™ 2 Platform, Enterprise Edition

Vlada Matena, Sanjeev Krishnan, Linda DeMichiel, Beth Stearns
Applying Enterprise JavaBeans™ 2.1, Second Edition: Component-Based Development for the J2EE™ Platform

Bill Shannon, Mark Hapner, Vlada Matena, James Davidson, Eduardo Pelegri-Llopart, Larry Cable, Enterprise Team
Java™ 2 Platform, Enterprise Edition: Platform and Component Specifications

Rahul Sharma, Beth Stearns, Tony Ng
J2EE™ Connector Architecture and Enterprise Application Integration

MIDP Style Guide

for the

Java™ 2 Platform, Micro Edition

Cynthia Bloch

Annette Wagner

♦♦Addison-Wesley

Boston • San Francisco • New York • Toronto • Montreal
London • Munich • Paris • Madrid
Capetown • Sydney • Tokyo • Singapore • Mexico City

Copyright © 2003 Sun Microsystems, Inc.
4150 Network Circle, Santa Clara, California 95054, U.S.A.
All rights reserved.

Sun Microsystems, Inc., has intellectual property rights relating to implementations of the technology described in this publication. In particular, and without limitation, these intellectual property rights may include one or more U.S. patents, foreign patents, or pending applications. Sun, Sun Microsystems, the Sun logo, J2ME, J2SE, Java Community Process, JCP, and all Sun and Java based trademarks and logos are trademarks or registered trademarks of Sun Microsystems, Inc., in the United States and other countries. UNIX is a registered trademark in the United States and other countries, exclusively licensed through X/Open Company, Ltd.

THIS PUBLICATION IS PROVIDED "AS IS" WITHOUT WARRANTY OF ANY KIND, EITHER EXPRESSED OR IMPLIED, INCLUDING, BUT NOT LIMITED TO, THE IMPLIED WARRANTIES OF MERCHANTABILITY, FITNESS FOR A PARTICULAR PURPOSE, OR NONINFRINGEMENT.

THIS PUBLICATION COULD INCLUDE TECHNICAL INACCURACIES OR TYPOGRAPHICAL ERRORS. CHANGES ARE PERIODICALLY ADDED TO THE INFORMATION HEREIN; THESE CHANGES WILL BE INCORPORATED IN NEW EDITIONS OF THE PUBLICATION. SUN MICROSYSTEMS, INC., MAY MAKE IMPROVEMENTS AND/OR CHANGES IN THE PRODUCT(S) AND/OR THE PROGRAM(S) DESCRIBED IN THIS PUBLICATION AT ANY TIME.

Library of Congress Cataloging-in-Publication Data is available.

The publisher offers discounts on this book when ordered in quantity for bulk purchases and special sales. For more information, please contact:
U.S. Corporate and Government Sales
(800) 382-3419
corpsales@pearsontechgroup.com

For sales outside of the U.S., please contact:
International Sales
(317) 581-3793
international@pearsontechgroup.com

Visit Addison-Wesley on the Web: www.awprofessional.com
ISBN: 0-321-19801-8
Text printed on recycled paper
1 2 3 4 5 6 7 8 9 10-CRS-0706050403
First printing, May 2003

To Eleanor and Robert O'Brien
— Annette

To Josh, Timothy, and Matthew Bloch
— Cindy

Contents

List of Figures

List of Tables

Preface

IF someone had told me that our world was going to be taken over by small devices back in 1995, I would have laughed. Then technology started moving in new directions—one of which was into cell phones. Cell phones not only take pictures but let me send those pictures to my mom if I so desire.

The world that opened up was one that enables people in many new, interesting and, sometimes, annoying ways. I'm still not sure I really *want* to get my email on my phone. After all, that seems to imply I should answer it right away, doesn't it?

At the first meeting of the minds on the Mobile Information Device Profile (MIDP), in January 2000, the issue of needing a style guide for this new technology was raised. Even then, all of us knew that if MIDP became successful, it would require a concerted effort from all the players: content providers, handset manufacturers, and operators. A style guide would help make that happen.

It took much longer than we expected to get the first version of the style guide out on the web. That's why, once the MIDP 2.0 effort began, we started planning for the second version of the style guide. It still took longer than we thought to get this book out. Murphy's Law works in mysterious ways.

We hope this book will educate our readers about MIDP as well as about user-experience issues. Creating great user interfaces is still as much science as it is art, and vice versa. If this book enables great MIDlets, it will be a success.

The focus here is on giving you as much advice as we can about what works and what doesn't work. Every domain has its idiosyncrasies and consumer user interface design is no different. If my company buys me a laptop and I don't like it, I grumble but use it. If I buy myself a cell phone and don't like it, it goes back to the store and I get my money back. That fundamental difference significantly changes people's motivation for what they will put up with. If you remember nothing else, remember that.

How This Book Is Organized

The *MIDP Style Guide* provides recommendations for designing the user interfaces of *MIDlets*, applications written in the Java™ programming language (Java applications) for MIDP. It guides user-interface (UI) designers, application developers, and MIDP implementors toward a common set of practices that are based on good UI and software design principles, user studies, and the specific requirements of MIDP. These practices will help designers, developers, and implementors create successful applications and devices.

To get the most out of this book, you should be familiar with the MIDP specifications. Both the *MIDP 1.0 Specification* [19] and the *MIDP 2.0 Specification* [19] are available from the Java Community Process℠ (JCP℠) at: http://jcp.org.

The following list describes the organization of the *MIDP Style Guide*:

- Chapter 1 provides an overview of the book's audience and typographical conventions. It also discusses consumer characteristics, consumer markets, and design considerations for consumer devices and applications.
- Chapter 2 describes the required device characteristics, as well as MIDP characteristics and their implications.
- Chapter 3 describes a design process for MIDP applications.
- Chapter 4 covers implementing and using high-level and low-level screens.
- Chapter 5 discusses implementing and using list screens.
- Chapter 6 covers implementing and using text boxes.
- Chapter 7 covers implementing and using forms, as well as form layout.
- Chapter 8 discusses implementing and using form items.
- Chapter 9 covers implementing and using alerts and alert types.
- Chapter 10 describes implementing and using canvases.
- Chapter 11 discusses implementing and using the new game package.
- Chapter 12 covers implementing and using abstract commands.
- Chapter 13 covers integrating MIDP and its applications into a device, and enabling users to download and install MIDlets over a network.
- Chapter 14 discusses implementing and using push functionality.
- Chapter 15 describes implementing and using the MIDP 2.0 security model.
- Chapter 16 covers using touch input, improving performance, and multi-threading.

Acknowledgments

WE would like to thank the many people who helped in the creation of this book. It's been a long journey, starting in 2000 with the initiation of the MIDP expert group, through putting version 1.0 on the web, to publishing the style guide as a book.

Our first set of thanks have to go to our respective teams—the User Experience and Documentation groups in J2ME land. The hours of reviewing, indexing, formatting, and image processing will not be forgotten. Special thanks to our manager, Rob Patten, for believing we could pull this off and getting us the support we needed to do so.

The entire MIDP team—East Coast, West Coast and Israel—for putting up with last-minute MIDlet changes and endless questions. Your support makes dreams come true.

And a huge note of thanks to our many external reviewers who come from many of the companies that comprise the MIDP expert group and beyond. Without your feedback, this book would not be as valuable as we hope it will be.

Last, but not least, thank you to the great folks at Addison-Wesley for putting up with our insane schedule.

CHAPTER 1

Introduction

M OBILE Information Device Profile (MIDP) defines the Java application environment for mobile information devices (MIDs), such as mobile phones and personal digital assistants (PDAs). MIDP is part of the Java™ 2 Platform, Micro Edition (J2ME™). This guide offers advice for MIDP 2.0, which is specified in *MIDP 2.0 Specification* [19] from the Mobile Information Device Profile 2.0 (JSR-000118).

An application that runs in the MIDP environment is called a *MIDlet*. One or more MIDlets packaged together for distribution are called a *MIDlet suite*.

This book is for two groups of readers: those who are porting MIDP to a new device (*MIDP implementors*) and those who are creating MIDlet suites (*application developers*). Porting MIDP implementations to devices and designing MIDlets both have special challenges, which this book's guidelines address.

The guidelines are divided into three categories. The following paragraphs show the typographical conventions used for the guidelines, and explain the guidelines themselves.

Strongly Recommend: Guidelines that, if not followed, could result in an unusable application.

Recommend: Guidelines that lead to an improved Java application in areas such as ease-of-use and portability. Disregarding this advice will not lead to an unusable application.

Consider: Guidelines that could lead to an improved Java application, but that do not necessarily apply to all applications and situations. Your circumstances may lead you to disregard this advice.

The guidelines come from many sources, including usability studies, user-interface design principles, good coding practices, and experience implementing the MIDP specification and MIDlets.

This chapter introduces design considerations for MIDlets in the consumer market. Designing MIDlets differs significantly from designing desktop computer software. Some important differences include product domain, resource limitations, and the need to focus on ease of use.

1.1   Consumer Characteristics

Consumer-application users have different characteristics than users of desktop systems. Consumers are familiar with appliances that typically have simple, predictable UIs, such as phones, microwave ovens, and remote controls, and might feel uncomfortable dealing with anything they consider too "high-tech." They expect consumer products to be predictable, easy to learn, and easy to use.

While electronic appliances are common today, widespread acceptance of new products is still hard fought. Eight of ten consumer products fail in the marketplace, often because consumers find them too difficult to use.

Application Developers and MIDP Implementors

 Recommend: Make new devices and applications as familiar, responsive, easy to learn, and easy to use as possible.

1.2   The Nature of Consumer Products

It is important to consider the limited resources and particular input and output (I/O) mechanisms of a consumer device because they typically have less memory, smaller or lower-resolution displays, fewer colors, and different I/O mechanisms than personal computers. Software and hardware must be tightly integrated.

MIDP Implementors

Consider: Integrate your MIDP implementation with the device's user experience. For example, coordinate the colors on the display with the colors of the physical components (such as the plastics), and the shape of the buttons on the screen with the shape of the physical buttons on the device. Strive to make using a MIDP application seem like using a *native application* (a resident application already installed on the device).

1.3   Consumer-Product Domains

Specialization for particular activities is a strength of consumer products such as televisions and mobile phones. Even products that might be used for multiple activities have a fundamental purpose. For example, a mobile phone is primarily a communications device, even though it may also include a few games. Devices that are compelling and successful in the marketplace have the right focus and features.

The focus of a device (the tasks it performs and the setting in which it is used) identifies its *domain*. For example, the domain of a basic pager is information access. Its tasks are receiving and displaying phone numbers or short text messages. It is used in short sessions and can be carried to any location. The consumer must be able to retrieve information (a phone number or a short message) quickly.

A product's domain has implications for the UI design and the user experience. There are many domains for consumer products. This section covers three that are relevant to MIDP.

1.3.1   Information Access and Communication

Mobile phones typify consumer products in the information access and communication domain. For example, consider a consumer using a web-enabled phone to find a particular restaurant, call it, and make reservations. Figure 1.1 shows how a consumer might interact with an application to perform this task.

Figure 1.1 Using a Web-Enabled Phone to Make Reservations

The information access and communication domain has the following characteristics.

- Products are used for:
  - Short periods at a time (a few seconds to five minutes)
  - Specific tasks
- Tasks:
  - Are usually structured and directed
  - Might be interrupted, but the interruptions are likely to be task relevant, such as getting a call while looking up a phone number
- Consumers:
  - Are likely to concentrate during their interactions
  - Approach the product with specific tasks or goals in mind
  - Are motivated to complete tasks and want quick, efficient, easy experiences
  - May be skeptical of the device's network connectivity
  - May doubt the device's ability to communicate properly at all times

The characteristics of this domain lead to the following design considerations.

Application Developers

Consider: Create UIs that provide efficient experiences. Task completion is important and time may be a critical factor. Consumers must be able to complete tasks quickly and efficiently.

 Recommend: Make screens work together. For example, an application should not return information to the consumer in one screen only to have the consumer enter it again a few screens later. It is inefficient and frustrating for a consumer to enter information that the application should already have.

 Recommend: Let the consumer know the outcome of an interaction that takes place across a network. It is obvious when some interactions have completed successfully. For example, when a browser requests a web page, the information exchange has obviously completed when the page is displayed. For other interactions, such as sending data to a remote location, the outcome might not be as obvious. Let consumers know that such data exchanges are progressing and when they are completed.

1.3.2   Business Functions

Products in the business functions domain help workers or operators perform very specific, job-related tasks. Examples include:

- Devices to help waiters take orders
- Applications to help assembly-line supervisors debug problems
- Devices to help delivery personnel plan routes and get customer signatures

These kinds of products can be thought of as vertical-market devices and applications because they target a specific task in a narrow field. Figure 1.2 shows an example application in this domain.

Figure 1.2   Using a PDA for Customer Signature Capture

The business functions domain has the following characteristics:

- Products are used for job-related tasks, for which training costs can be an issue
- Tasks are such that interruptions are possible but are likely to be task relevant
- Tasks might be completed incrementally
- Consumers usually have domain knowledge specific to the application

The characteristics and design implications of the business functions domain are similar to those of the information access and communication domain; however, applications in this domain need to be efficient and predictable. (See "Information Access and Communication" on page 3.)

1.3.3   Entertainment

Playing a game on a mobile phone while standing in line at the grocery store exemplifies an interaction in the entertainment domain; for example, see Figure 1.3.

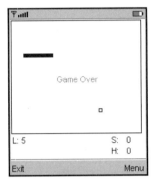

Figure 1.3   Using a Mobile Phone to Play a Game

Consumer products used for entertainment, such as games on PDAs or gaming devices, share these characteristics:

- Products are used:
    - In comfortable, low-stress environments
    - For 10 to 30 minutes or more at a time
    - For less structured tasks
- Tasks are such that interruptions are possible
- Consumers:
    - Are likely to have varying levels of concentration and attention during their interactions
    - Approach the products with a relaxed attitude
    - Are more interested in a pleasant experience than in performing a specific task

Design considerations for the entertainment domain include the following.

Application Developers and MIDP Implementors

 Recommend: Create UIs that interfere as little as possible with the content. For example, an application's controls should take up as little screen real estate as possible so that consumers can see more of the screen. Consumers will have various levels of concentration. Forcing consumers to concentrate on the UI will make their experience with the product less enjoyable.

Application Developers

Consider: Create entertainment UIs that provide a pleasant experience in preference to an efficient one. Task completion time in this domain is not a critical factor because the consumer is not under significant time pressure.

Efficiency is a positive attribute, but in the entertainment domain, a pleasant and compelling experience is as important as efficiency. Predictability, however, is more important than efficiency.

Consider: Devote as much I/O bandwidth as possible to seeing, hearing, and interacting with the entertainment. The interaction of the consumer and the game is the product's most important feature.

1.4   Design Considerations for Consumer Products

Some principles for designing consumer-product UIs are independent of the product's domain. This section covers some of these principles. See *Information Appliances and Beyond: Interaction Design for Consumer Products* [1] for more information.

1.4.1   Simplify

Simplifying UIs is an objective for all designers. For consumer products, you can make a trade-off of functionality and choice against simplicity.

1.4.2   Functionality Versus Simplicity

The more functionality included in a product, the more difficult it is to learn and to use. On the other hand, gratuitous elimination of functionality can lead to a product that is too limited to support consumers' needs. Strive for the *functionality threshold*—the right collection and number of features to strike a balance between functionality and simplicity.

Application Developers and MIDP Implementors

Recommend: Use the 80/20 rule: Identify the 20 percent of the functionality that will meet 80 percent of the consumers' needs and optimize your design accordingly. After you have supported 80 percent of the consumers' needs, you can decide what, if any, of the remaining functionality to include based on other criteria (such as competitive edge and price). Do not change your design to provide the same level of access to these functions as to the critical functionality.

1.4.3   Choice Versus Simplicity

Choice is useful when it is appropriate, but too much choice can create a complicated, perhaps overwhelming, situation. For example, consider replying to an email. An email application could give you the choice of replying to the sender and including the original mail in the reply, replying to the sender without including the original mail, replying to everyone who received the original mail and including the original mail in the reply, and replying to everyone who received the original mail without including it in the reply.

Application Developers and MIDP Implementors

Consider: Reduce choice by providing reasonable defaults and removing nonessential options. For example, MIDlet suites can contain one or more MIDlets. A MIDlet suite containing multiple MIDlets forces the consumer to choose which MIDlet to run. If a MIDlet suite contains a single MIDlet, a MIDlet implementation could simply launch the suite, relieving the consumer of having to "choose" from a single element list. A MIDlet implementation that removes that choice point has a simpler design and meets consumers needs.

1.4.4   Make It Predictable

Usability testing has shown that consumers are much happier with systems that are predictable, even at the cost of efficiency.

Application Developers and MIDP Implementors

 Strongly Recommend: Design your MIDP implementation or MIDlet so that consumers can predict what will happen when they take an action. Consumers rarely read documentation.

For example, assume that an address book application and an email application on a mobile phone have menus that display the available operations, and the address book has a menu element called New Entry for adding a record. The question for the email application is whether its list element for writing a new message should be called Write or New Message. Using New Message is parallel to New Entry in the address book, which makes it an attractive option. It makes the address book and email applications more consistent. Consumers, though, do not think about creating a new message; they think of writing to someone. For them, Write would probably be a better predictor of the command's behavior.

 Recommend: If you must choose between predictable and efficient, choose predictable. Predictability is a better investment than efficiency.

MIDP Implementors

 Recommend: Publish the runtime behavior of your MIDP implementation. This will help developers understand the conventions and behavior of your device so that they are better able to make their MIDlets predictable to users of your device.

1.4.5   Streamline Important Tasks for Efficiency

Application Developers and MIDP Implementors

Recommend: Minimize the amount of navigation and user interaction required to complete frequent or crucial tasks. These operations should require as little overhead as possible.

When you consider this recommendation remember that predictability is more important than efficiency in a consumer product.

One way to minimize navigation is to design applications with shallow hierarchies so that consumers do not find themselves going from screen to screen to screen, and then back, back, back.

Application Developers

Consider: If an application requires a sequence of steps from which consumers may need to retreat, enable them to go back multiple steps at a time in addition to returning to the previous screen.

1.4.6   Make It Responsive

Consumers expect immediate response to their input. When a response is not immediate, they can become annoyed, repeatedly press buttons, or assume the device is broken. They may stop using the device.

Application Developers and MIDP Implementors

Strongly Recommend: Have the device respond so that consumers are confident that each of their actions was received. For example, the device could confirm button presses with a click sound and in some circumstances an application might use visual feedback to tell consumers the system got their input.

Strongly Recommend: Avoid blank screens. Consumers think that a product is faster if things keep happening on the screen, as opposed to not showing anything until an operation is done.

Strongly Recommend: Minimize delays and if there is a delay give appropriate feedback. For example, display an animated indicator when downloading information, preferably one that shows how the operation is progressing. Providing dynamic feedback to consumers during delays keeps them engaged.

Responsiveness starts with immediate feedback and goes beyond it to intelligent responses.

MIDP Implementors

Consider: Have the product respond to common activities in a way that makes life easier for the consumer. For example, launching an application is a common activity. If a MIDlet suite contains a single MIDlet, it makes the consumer's life easier if the device automatically runs the MIDlet when the consumer launches the MIDlet suite (as mentioned previously).

1.4.7   Provide Constant, Unobtrusive Feedback

The users of consumer products need reassurance that the device is functioning correctly, even when nothing important is going on.

MIDP Implementors

 Strongly Recommend: Ensure that something on the screen always shows that the product is on. The indicator should not be annoying or distracting. It could be something like a connection graphic or a power light.

For example, most mobile phones have a signal strength indicator, which is active when the phone is on. Its feedback is crucial when making phone calls. The indicator is positioned so that it does not interfere with the display of other information. Figure 1.4 shows the signal strength indicator in the MIDP Reference Implementation.

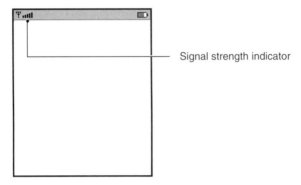

Figure 1.4 Signal Strength Feedback on a Mobile Phone

Application Developers and MIDP Implementors

> *Consider*: Animation and sound can convey feedback to the consumer. In some cases, a slow animation might be more unobtrusive than other types of feedback. For example, an animation indicating that a product is connected to a network does not have to change quickly; it is more effective at a slow, even pace.

Figure 1.5 shows the images for a slow, even animation that indicates network activity.

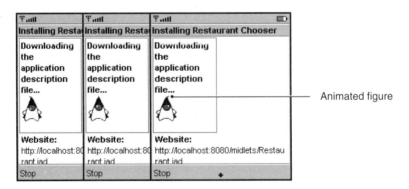

Figure 1.5 Animation Indicating Activity

1.4.8 Make Everything Interruptible

Consumers should *always* be able to cancel, power off, or simply interrupt the device in order to do something else, even when there is a message that requires a response on the screen or they are in the middle of a task. If a person is in the middle of an activity, the consumer should be able to start over at the beginning of that activity without penalty.

Application Developers and MIDP Implementors

Strongly Recommend: Enable consumers to interrupt an application no matter what state it is in.

For example, when a PDA shows a *modal alert* (a message on a screen that the user must dismiss), the consumer should be able to dismiss it not only by tapping a particular button but also by tapping outside the alert. Similarly, if a consumer is writing an email message and wants to go to another application, the device should automatically save the message as a draft without displaying error messages or prompts.

Allowing a user to interrupt anything keeps control of the product in the hands of the consumer. People are more comfortable with products they control.

1.4.9 Minimize Interruptions From MIDP and MIDlets

Consumers should not be interrupted and required to respond unless it is absolutely necessary. Confirmation messages, unnecessary feedback, and error messages that require a response detract from the user experience.

Application Developers and MIDP Implementors

Consider: Restrict interruptions to critical information.

Consider: Use less-obtrusive mechanisms, such as a *timed alert*, for providing feedback that is not critical. A timed alert is a screen with a message for the user; it is visible briefly and does not require a response. For example, if the consumer is in a Preferences screen and presses Save, a timed alert could be used to confirm that the preferences were saved.

It can be difficult to decide when a particular piece of information is critical. For example, consider consumers downloading applications onto mobile phones. If network connections are lost, the losses can be considered critical information that lets consumers know that they should reconnect. Another approach, though, is to have the devices automatically try to reconnect and unobtrusively display that status. The second approach keeps interruptions to a minimum. When deciding how to handle this situation, consider the cost to the consumer for the connection, as well as the consumer's time.

Application Developers and MIDP Implementors, Continued

 Strongly Recommend: When using modal alerts to give consumers critical information, do not make the device appear to be broken. Use plain language to explain the problem. Test your error messages with real consumers.

This approach allows consumers to decipher critical information and maintains their confidence in the device.

1.4.10   Check Your Designs with Others

In any design process, it is valuable to periodically check your designs against the wants and expectations of your audience. You could do this by comparing your design to product-marketing requirements, visiting prospective customers, and evaluating competing products.

Application Developers and MIDP Implementors

Consider: Involving consumers in exploratory studies, blank model studies, and surveys are some of the best ways to check how well consumers like your product design. (Blank model studies allow consumers to design a product from scratch, without being given a design to start with. They remove a designer's preconceptions from the consumers' view.)

See "Bibliography" on page 243 for sources of information on these techniques.

CHAPTER 2

MIDP Characteristics

THE characteristics of devices and the MIDP environment have important implications for MIDP implementors and application designers. This chapter covers not only those characteristics and implications, but also summarizes the changes from MIDP 1.0 to MIDP 2.0.

2.1 Characteristics of MIDs

According to the *MIDP 2.0 Specification* [19], a MID should have these *minimum* hardware characteristics:

- Display
  - Screen size of 96-by-54 pixels
  - Display depth of 1 bit
  - Pixel shape (aspect ratio) of approximately 1:1
- Input – one-handed keyboard (ITU-T phone keypad), two-handed keyboard, (QWERTY keyboard), or touch screen
- Memory
  - 256 kilobytes of nonvolatile memory for the MIDP components
  - 8 kilobytes of nonvolatile memory for application-created persistent data
  - 128 kilobytes of volatile memory for the Java runtime environment
- Networking
  - Two-way
  - Wireless

- Possibly intermittent

- Limited bandwidth

• Sound – ability to play tones, either via dedicated hardware, or via software algorithm

Example MIDs are mobile phones, two-way pagers, and wireless-enabled personal digital assistants (PDAs). Table 2.1 has some general system characteristics.

Table 2.1: Platform Characteristics

Characteristic	Mobile Phone	PDA
Applications	Telephony, voice mail, address book, web browser, text messaging	Address book, to-do list, calendar, memo pad
Input device	Keypad buttons	Touch, stylus, QWERTY keyboard, IR
Mouse support	None	None
Keyboard support	Phone ITU-T keypad	Onscreen keyboard, QWERTY keyboard
Viewing distance	6 inches to 2 feet	1 to 2 feet
Display size	1-by-2 inches	2-by-2 inches
Screen resolution	A range that includes 96x54	A range that includes 160x160
Screen colors	Black and white through 16-bit color displays	Black and white through 16-bit color displays
Pixel density	72 to 102 or more DPI	72 to 102 or more DPI
Multiple screens	No	No
Audio input	Available	Available
Audio output	Speaker, headset	Speaker, headphones
Data bandwidth	14.4Kbps to 3Gbps	14.4Kbps to 3Gbps
Desktop synchronization	Available	Available
Bluetooth or serial network capabilities	Available	Available
Camera	Available	Available

2.2   Changes from MIDP 1.0 to MIDP 2.0

The *MIDP 2.0 Specification* [19] enhances and extends the *MIDP 1.0 Specification* [19]. The *MIDP 2.0 Specification* adds the following functionality to MIDP.

- Application delivery and installation (over-the-air provisioning was only a recommended practice in MIDP 1.0)
- Application signing model and privileged domains security model
- Support for receiving pushed data
- Networking – In addition to the MIDP 1.0 HTTP API, MIDP 2.0 has:
  - HTTPS
  - Comm
  - Datagram
  - Sockets
  - Server sockets
- Sound
- Timers
- New UI components:
  - CustomItem
  - Pop-up choice group
  - Spacer
  - Game canvas
- Graphics – Has new capabilities, such as copying an area from one place on a graphic to another
- Updated form and form items (the following list provides highlights, but is not an exhaustive list of changes.)
  - ChoiceGroup – A MIDlet can now request a text policy (e.g., `TEXT_WRAP_ON`) and specify fonts
  - Form – New layout policy
  - Gauge – Can now specify states for the gauge, such as `CONTINUOUS_RUNNING`
  - ImageItem – Has new appearance modes, such as `BUTTON` and `HYPERLINK`

- Item – Can now specify a minimum height and width, a preferred height and width, and a layout directive (layout directives were only for image items in MIDP 1.0)

- StringItem – Has new appearance modes, such as BUTTON and HYPERLINK

- TextField – Has new constraints (such as DECIMAL) and new modifiers (such as UNEDITABLE)

• Other updated UI components:

- Alert – Can have commands and a gauge

- Canvas – Has a full-screen mode: can have a ticker

- Choice – Has a new type of choice (pop-up) and new text policies (such as TEXT_WRAP_ON)

- Command – Can now have a short and a long label

- Display – Has backlight and vibrate functionality

- Displayable – Has ticker and title

- Image – Can now handle transparency

- Lists – Implicit lists can specify a default command

- Screen – The ticker and title commands were moved from here to Displayable

- TextBox – TextField's updates affect TextBox

- Ticker – Can now be attached to a Displayable

2.3   Characteristics of the MIDP Environment

The MIDP environment is networked, screen-based, and secure. Network capability does not need to be constant; a device could be connected to a network only intermittently.

2.3.1   Screen-Based Environment

In MIDP's screen-based environment, application designers use screens to organize their user interfaces into manageable tasks. (See Chapter 3 for more information.) MIDP implementations control the look and layout of screen components. Consumers interact on a screen-by-screen basis with their applications.

All screens are part of *LCDUI*, the user-interface components of MIDP. The package was designed for devices with small screens and limited or absent windowing capability. For example, unlike Java 2 Platform, Standard Edition (J2SE™) user-interface packages (such as Swing), LCDUI does not provide overlapping windows; it is not a desktop user-interface toolkit.

There are two categories of LCDUI screens: *structured* and *unstructured*. Structured screens are more portable, but do not give the application access to low-level input mechanisms or control of the screen. Unstructured screens provide access to low-level I/O, but can be less portable.

Structured screens are created using the LCDUI *high-level* APIs, which provide user-interface components such as lists and forms. See Chapter 5 through Chapter 9 for more information.

Unstructured screens are created using the LCDUI *low-level* APIs, which provide access to low-level device I/O. Because I/O is device-specific, applications written with the low-level APIs are not guaranteed to be portable. For example, it is possible to use an unstructured screen to write an application that depends on a touch screen. This type of application is not portable to all devices, only to devices with touch screens. Chapter 10 and Chapter 11 contain advice to help application designers create portable applications using the low-level APIs.

2.3.2   Security Features

The MIDP 2.0 environment also has security features: MIDlets require permission to access security-sensitive APIs. A *trusted* MIDlet suite (one for which the device can trust the origin and integrity of the JAR file) can be granted permission to use these APIs. It is up to the device to determine whether a MIDlet suite is trusted. Untrusted MIDlet suites are either denied permission to the security-sensitive APIs or can access them after getting permission from the user. See Chapter 15 for more information.

2.4   Implications of the MIDP Environment

Usability studies on consumer products have repeatedly shown that predictability (having the product "do the right thing" on the device) is far more important than consistency or efficiency. Forcing consistency across radically different products often makes the products unusable.

2.4.1   Device-Specific MIDP Implementations

With many programming languages, making applications predictable across multiple devices requires porting the application from device to device, with each version of the application using different user-interface code. This would be especially difficult for mobile information devices because of the many types of device displays and input-output solutions. With MIDP, applications do not control the details of focus, traversal, scrolling, and so on. Those device-specific details are handled by the MIDP implementation. As a result, well-designed MIDP applications can run on multiple devices without code changes, which saves time.

Giving MIDP implementors the responsibility of creating and laying out MIDP user-interface components for their devices also enables applications to look and act like device-native applications on multiple devices without code changes. When a MIDP application looks and acts like a device-native application, it is predictable. Predictable applications are easier to learn and use.

MIDP Implementors

 Strongly Recommend: Create and lay out MIDP user-interface components in a way that enables MIDlets to look as much like native applications as possible. For example, assume that a device has a particular way to present a list to the consumer. The MIDP implementor should ensure that the MIDP implementation presents lists in the same way (within the bounds of the MIDP specification).

Consider, for example, an address book on a mobile phone with a 100-by-128, four-level grayscale display and an ITU-T phone keypad. The application could have a vertical layout with two soft buttons on the bottom of the screen. Now, move the address book to a device that has a stylus, touch screen, and 240-by-100 pixel, 256-color display. If the application were responsible for the details of the UI, the vertical layout would be awkward and inappropriate. Instead, assuming that the MIDlet has both color and grayscale graphics, it could look and behave as if it were created for the second device, without code changes. Figure 2.1 shows a mock-up of the application on the two devices.

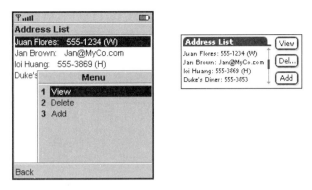

Figure 2.1 Alternate, Device-Dependant Layouts for an Application

In addition to making the screens look like those of native applications, MIDP implementors can also make MIDP user-interface components behave in ways that are similar to native applications.

MIDP Implementors

Strongly Recommend: If your device supports touch input, incorporate it into your MIDP screens in a way that is consistent with the capabilities of native applications. For example, you could allow a user to choose an element of a list by tapping it.

Strongly Recommend: If your device has keys or gestures dedicated to certain tasks, such as selection, use the same keys for MIDP tasks.

2.4.2   Device-Independent Application Design

Application Developers

Recommend: Ensure your applications are predictable. For example, always have your unstructured screens support key presses, a standard input mechanism. In addition, add touch input capabilities if the device supports them. See Chapter 10 for more information.

2.4.3   Network-Sensitive Application Design

Application Developers

Recommend: Always consider cost and latency for networked applications. Consumers might pay for airtime by the minute or packet. Requiring a constant network connection could make your application costly to run. In addition, in current mobile phone networks a round trip to and from a server could take two seconds or longer. High latencies affect responsiveness. For example, a fast-paced two-player game would be unusable under these circumstances.

CHAPTER 3

Designing Applications for MIDP

DESIGNING MIDlets differs from designing desktop applications because the MIDP environment is screen-based, not window-based or command-line oriented. The screen-based environment requires more consideration of application flow. This chapter provides an overview of a MIDlet design process. (See *Designing from Both Sides of the Screen: How Designers and Engineers Can Collaborate to Build Cooperative Technology* [5] for more information.)

3.1   Characterizing the Application

It is important for a MIDlet to have a clearly defined purpose. Characterizing the application is an application designer's first opportunity to express that purpose.

Application Developers

Recommend: In the early stages of MIDlet design, characterize the application with a one-sentence description of what it will enable consumers to do. Consider the high-level purpose of the MIDlet before defining any lower-level tasks. For example, *SmartTicket*, a movie ticket application, could be described this way: "This application enables consumers to buy movie tickets from their connected device."

SmartTicket, the example used throughout this book, is a MIDlet available from the BluePrints group. (See `http://java.sun.com/blueprints/code/` for one version of SmartTicket [22].)

3.2   Describing a Usage Case

A usage case is a "story" about what consumers will do with the application. The story will help determine the MIDlet's tasks at a lower level. The usage case should not describe how users operate the device.

Application Developers

 Recommend: Use the one-sentence description and, if possible, use data collected from target users, to write a usage case for your MIDlet.

For example, the story for SmartTicket might be something like this:

> Tony likes to go to movies and would like to be able to buy movie tickets without having to stand in line at the theater, even when he is not at his computer.
>
> Tony uses SmartTicket because he can easily see what movies are in his area and find out where and when they are playing.
>
> Today when Tony checked on movies, the application showed him a new first-run movie, *The Invasion of the Dots*, that he wanted to see. He found that it was playing at a theater near his house at a convenient time. Tony bought a ticket and chose the seat that he wanted in the theater.

3.3   Identifying Tasks

Tasks are the activities users perform in order to achieve their goals. Tasks are described in terms of what the user is trying to accomplish, not in terms of a particular implementation or UI flow.

 Recommend: Derive tasks from your use case. Once you have identified a core set of tasks from your initial use case, you can build on it with more tasks that make sense as part of your list. Don't try to organize the tasks at this point; in the next step, you will begin to do that and to conceptualize the UI structure.

For example, a partial list of tasks for SmartTicket might look something like this:

- Choose a movie
- Rate movies
- Find a theater
- Buy tickets
- View movie show times

3.4   Sketching Tasks

Application Developers

Recommend: Map the story to a series of sketches that represent users' tasks. Use a pencil or another erasable writing device so that you can quickly and easily revise your screen layouts, terminology, and overall design.

When you map the story to sketches, do not consider low-level details such as how users will operate the device. Concentrate on the purpose of the story and the tasks the user should be able to perform. For example, SmartTicket could be made up in part of the sketches in Table 3.1

Note that the sketches do not show navigational devices such as scroll bars and buttons.

Table 3.1: Early Sketches of SmartTicket

Sketch	Location in the Story	Tasks in the Sketch
	At application launch	None. The sketch simply shows a Splash screen that goes away after a few seconds to reveal the application.
High-level task list for the application 	After the Splash screen (when the device owner already has an account)	• Choose a movie • Rate movies • Update your account • Update the theater schedules available on your device • Exit the application

Sketch	Location in the Story	Tasks in the Sketch
Choosing a movie 	After the initial screen when the user chooses the Choose Movie option	• Choose a theater • Choose a movie • Choose a time • Request a seating preference • Select the number of tickets to buy • Show a preview • Choose a movie by seeing a list of movies • See which movies will be coming soon • Rate movies you have seen • Update your account • See an About box

Recommend: Share your sketches with others to ensure your design is meeting consumers' needs. While the sketches are not a full representation of the final application, they should be complete enough to share with marketing professionals, consumers, and others in an informal manner. Sharing your sketches also enables you to check expectations. When you have a conversation about what consumers want, you can check whether your application provides it (or can easily be modified to provide it).

3.5   Designing Application Flow

When the sketches are satisfactory, the application flow will emerge from them.

Application Developers

Recommend: Use your sketches to trace the flow through the MIDlet and ensure you have minimized the interaction required for frequent tasks.

3.6   Creating a Mock-Up

Application Developers

Recommend: Map your sketches to a set of screens, each of which enables the consumer to carry out one or more tasks. The screens should show the user-interface components of MIDP. This activity refines the sketches into a mock-up of the application.

The mock-up of the application should include navigational devices that a MIDP implementor might use. The remaining chapters help with this task by providing recommendations on how best to use *LCDUI*, the user-interface components of MIDP.

The mock-up will have more screens than there were sketches because it will include screens for any busy indicators in the application and for any *system menus* (lists or menus generated by the MIDP implementation) that a device might use. For example, MIDP implementors often map *abstract commands* to system menus, so the mock-up could contain these screens. (Abstract commands are actions that have an interface determined by the MIDP implementation instead of being associated with a specific UI component such as a list. The following actions on the SmartTicket sketch for choosing a movie are abstract commands: showing a preview, seeing a list of movies, seeing which movies will be coming soon, rating movies, updating the user's account, and seeing an About box. See Chapter 12 for more information.)

Figure 3.1 shows part of an early mock-up for SmartTicket, going from the Splash screen to a list of high-level tasks, then to a form for choosing a movie. The form happens to be drawn as four separate pictures, and shows the abstract commands on the last screen.

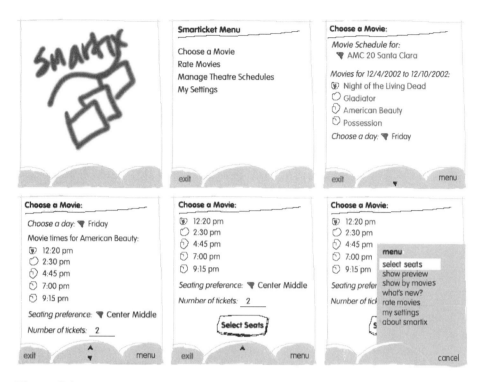

Figure 3.1 Partial Mock-up for SmartTicket

 Recommend: Use the mock-up to further study, test, and share your designs.

It is important to note that when the application is implemented, its screens will be laid out by the MIDP implementation on the device. Because MIDP implementations should strive to follow the conventions of the device, the application may or may not look like the mock-up. For example, Table 3.2 shows the SmartTicket screens that correspond to the mock-up on a mobile phone.

Table 3.2: Comparison of Mock-up and an Implementation

Screen Mock-up	Screen on a Mobile Phone

Screen Mock-up	Screen on a Mobile Phone

CHAPTER 4

Screen Layout

OBJECTS shown on the screen are *displayables*. Displayables include both structured and unstructured screens. See "Characteristics of the MIDP Environment" on page 18 for more information on structured and unstructured screens, and *Programming Wireless Devices with the Java™ 2 Platform, Micro Edition* [17] for information on the Displayable API.

Displayables can have a title and a ticker and should have one or more abstract commands. (See Chapter 12 for more information on abstract commands.) Displayables might also have additional elements, such as activity indicators for network activity, battery life, and scrolling. This chapter has advice for laying out these elements.

Application Developer Responsibilities	MIDP Implementor Responsibilities

• Any text to be used in the ticker
• Any text to be used in the screen's title
• For an unstructured screen, whether to use *full-screen mode*, which removes any title or ticker to maximize the portion of the screen available to the application
	• Fonts and colors used on the screen
	• Support for a title
	  • Screen location
	  • Text-display policy (for example, will title-text be wrapped or clipped)
	• Support for a ticker
	  • Screen location
	  • Ticker size
	  • Ticker font
	  • Direction of scroll
	  • Scroll rate
	• Location of any onscreen indicators
	• Backlight support
	• Vibrate capability
	• Abstract command support

4.1   Tickers and Titles

While the *MIDP 2.0 Specification* allows unstructured screens to have tickers and titles, structured screens have always had the ability to include a ticker and a title. A screen has the general layout, as shown in Figure 4.1. The placement of these two components is device-specific.

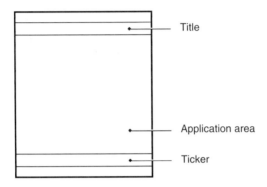

Figure 4.1   Screen Layout

MIDP Implementors

Strongly Recommend: Place the title and ticker in the same place on both a structured screen and an unstructured screen. This gives users visual continuity as they move from one screen to another in an application. Figure 4.2 shows the titles and the tickers on structured and unstructured screens in the MIDP Reference Implementation.

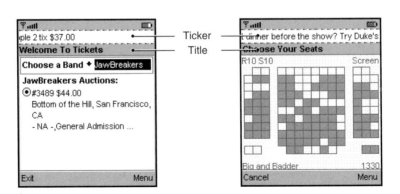

Figure 4.2   Titles and Tickers on Structured and Unstructured Screens

Consider: If your device is accessible to people with disabilities, consider providing a way for users to change the scroll rate of the ticker, and the fonts used on the device, including fonts for the title and the ticker.

 Recommend: Use your device's global font settings instead of creating a MIDP-only setting.

Application Developers

Consider: You can insert, delete, or change the title and the ticker as required by your application.

4.1.1   Handling Long Titles

MIDP Implementors

 Recommend: If you allow multiline titles, wrap text on word boundaries, wrap words longer than one line on character boundaries, and include the *white space* requested by the application. (White space is defined as spaces and carriage returns; including requested white space is called *honoring white space*.) Text is most readable if it breaks on word boundaries. For example, users find titles like the one in Figure 4.3, which do not wrap on word boundaries, disconcerting. Application developers may use white space to improve readability; applications will be more usable if the device honors this white space.

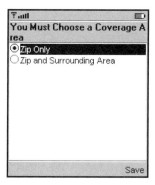

Figure 4.3 Not Recommended: Title Does Not Wrap on Word Boundaries

Strongly Recommend: If you must clip titles due to device restrictions, indicate that the label has been shortened. A common way to indicate clipping is by using an *ellipsis* (. . .), as shown in Figure 4.4.

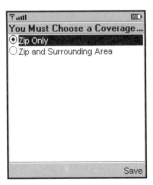

Figure 4.4   Clipped Title Shown with an Ellipsis

4.1.2   System-Generated Screens

MIDP Implementors

Consider: If an item cannot be edited on the form, but instead must be edited on a new screen, consider using the item label as the title of the new screen. (Using a new, system-generated screen to edit a form item is called editing *off the form*.) A label should act as a prompt for an interactive item (as recommended on page 87). Using the item label as the title of the Editing screen helps the user retain context. When the screen title reminds the user of the purpose of the Editing screen, user error is reduced.

Consider: If you create a new screen for editing off the form, that new screen should not contain any ticker that was on the original screen.

4.2   Onscreen Indicators

In addition to the title and ticker, a MIDP implementation can also reserve screen space for other purposes. For example, the MIDP Reference Implementation also renders a signal strength indicator, battery indicator, trust indicator (see Chapter 15 for more information), input mode indicator (see Chapter 6 for more information), scroll indicator, and the labels of abstract commands (see Chapter 12). It could, but does not, put a network activity indicator on the screen. Figure 4.5 points out these indicators and labels.

Within some contexts, a volume indicator also may be helpful.

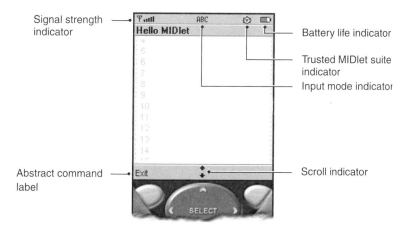

Figure 4.5 Reference Implementation Indicators and Labels

MIDP Implementors

Strongly Recommend: Follow your device conventions as much as possible when designing the layout of your MIDP screens. Consistency among Java applications and native applications makes using MIDlets a more predictable experience for users.

Consider: Include an indicator that turns on when a MIDlet uses airtime. (All MIDP implementations must provide a visual network-usage indicator. If your device has such an indicator on its body, that is sufficient to satisfy the *MIDP 2.0 Specification* [19].)

Strongly Recommend: If you provide an onscreen network-usage indicator or a trust indicator, do not put them in the application area. For security, these indicators should not be controlled by the Java application. Instead, put them in a part of the screen that is controlled by the system.

4.3   Full-Screen Mode

Unstructured screens can be displayed in *full-screen mode*. (See Chapter 10 for more information on unstructured screens, including when an application might use full-screen mode.) In full-screen mode, the MIDP implementation does not show any title or ticker, but it might still show indicators.

MIDP Implementors

 Strongly Recommend: Do not allow full-screen mode to take over any area used to display security-related information, such as a trust indicator. If your implementation gives this area to the application, a MIDlet in full-screen mode could display its own trusted icon and trick the user into thinking that it is trusted when it is not.

 Recommend: If your screen layout includes labels for soft buttons, do not hide them in full-screen mode. If you do need to hide them, display them in response to a user pressing either soft button.

 Recommend: Although you must not display the title when an unstructured screen is in full-screen mode, you can use the text of the title for related items, such as system menus.

Application Developers

Consider: You can change an unstructured screen to and from full-screen mode at any time. (Changing to and from full-screen mode at arbitrary times isn't a good idea, however; see Chapter 10 for more information.)

CHAPTER 5

Lists

A LIST is a screen of choices. MIDP offers three list types: *exclusive-choice*, which allows the user to select one and only one element; *multiple-choice*, which allows the user to select zero or more elements; and *implicit*, which allows the user to select one element for a subsequent action. Figure 5.1 shows the three list types.

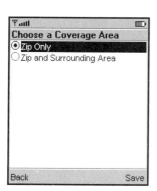 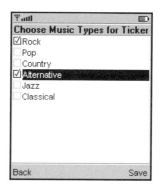 

Figure 5.1 Exclusive-Choice, Multiple-Choice, and Implicit Lists

Application Developer Responsibilities	MIDP Implementor Responsibilities
• Abstract commands for the screen (not required for implicit lists) • Text associated with each element • Image, if any, for each element • Requested font, if any, for each element • Requested text handling (wrapped or not) • Preselected element or elements (a list-dependent number)	• Default font and color • Text-display policy (wrapped, clipped, or scroll-through) • Element height • Default starting position of traversal highlight • How users traverse and scroll • How to indicate element selection • Legal image size for a list item • How users select an element • Giving the application a user's final selection

5.1   Working with Lists

How you work with and display lists is independent of list type. Factors include managing and displaying list items, the content of list titles, element selection, and so on. This section covers those pieces of advice.

MIDP Implementors

 Recommend: Publish your policy decisions, such as text display and the size of graphics you permit in lists. This way, application developers can take them into account when they create their MIDlets.

5.1.1   Managing List Elements

A list can contain one or more elements, each of which can be comprised of text, a graphic, or both. The application developer provides the list elements and can insert, delete, update, select, and deselect list elements as needed. (See *Programming Wireless Devices with the Java™ 2 Platform, Micro Edition* [17] for information on the List API.)

Application Developers

 Strongly Recommend: Do not change a list's contents while the list is visible, except in response to a user action, such as selecting an element. Making arbitrary changes while the user is interacting with the list is disorienting, but users understand context-sensitive screens that change in response to their actions.

 Recommend: Do not change a list's selection while the list is visible. It is possible to change which list element is selected, even while the list screen is visible, but it can be disorienting. For example, the highlighting could appear to jump around on the screen. Odd behavior like this can result in user errors.

5.1.2   Displaying Lists

When users are required to traverse elements on the screen in order to reach the one they want, the device must provide a visual indicator of the user's current position (or *focus*). In exclusive- and multiple-choice lists, a highlight can indicate the user's focus without indicating selection. For example, in Figure 5.2 if the user selects Save, the selections indicated by the check-box graphic, not the highlight, will be saved.

In implicit lists, a highlight indicates both the user's focus and element selection. For example, in Figure 5.3 if the user presses the Select button, the action will be carried out on the selection indicated by the highlight.

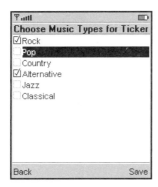

Figure 5.2   Highlighting That Shows Focus, Not Selection

Figure 5.3   Highlighting That Shows Focus and Selection

MIDP Implementors

Consider: Use a visual indicator to show that a list element in an exclusive- or multiple-choice list is selected. Radio buttons and check boxes are commonly used for this purpose.

Strongly Recommend: If you use a graphic, such as a radio button to indicate that a list element is selected, its size should be consistent with the policy of your device. For usability, it should be at least 12 pixels high by 12 pixels wide.

Strongly Recommend: Do not extend a list element's highlighting over any associated graphic or image. A highlight extending over a graphic or image, especially when the highlight reverses the foreground and background (*reverse video*), can result in a confusing visual display. It can be difficult to determine the state of the graphic when it has been reversed. Users can make mistakes if it is not clear whether the highlighted item is selected. Figure 5.4 shows that, when the graphic is not highlighted, the user's selection is clear.

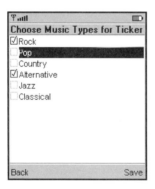 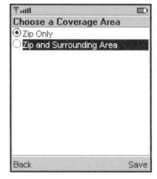

Figure 5.4 No Reverse-Video Highlighting on the Graphic or Image

5.1.3   List Titles

Application Developers

Recommend: As shown Figure 5.5, use the title of the list screen to tell users what they need to do on the screen.

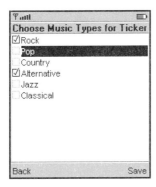

Figure 5.5 Screen Title That Instructs Users

5.1.4   Element Selection

MIDP Implementors

Strongly Recommend: You must provide a way for users to select list elements. If your device has a dedicated hardware Select or Go key, use it for the select operation. If your device does not have a dedicated key, you must provide another method, such as using a soft-key or touch-screen input.

Recommend: If you use a soft key for the select operation, consider providing a label of Select for exclusive-choice lists; a label of Mark or Unmark for multiple-choice lists; and either the MIDlet's label or a label of Select or Go if the MIDlet doesn't provide a label for an implicit list. (The *MIDP 2.0 Specification* [19] recommends that application developers label commands associated with implicit lists. See "Implicit Lists" on page 48 for more information.)

Strongly Recommend: Notify the application of a user's selection when the user indicates that the selection is final.

5.1.5   Text Handling

Applications can suggest a preferred text-handling method for a list element's contents. Possible methods are:

- TEXT_WRAP_OFF: text element contents should be limited to a single line.

- TEXT_WRAP_ON: text element contents should be wrapped to multiple lines if necessary to fit available content space.

- TEXT_WRAP_DEFAULT: the implementation should use its default behavior.

MIDP Implementors

Strongly Recommend: Choose and publish the default text-handling method for your device.

Strongly Recommend: If an element requests TEXT_WRAP_OFF, you might have to shorten its contents to fit on a line. If you shorten the text, give users a visual indication, such as an ellipsis, to indicate that the text has been clipped.

Recommend: If an element requests TEXT_WRAP_OFF and the contents don't fit on a line, provide a way for users to see the full element contents. This may be done, for example, by using a special pop-up window or by auto-scrolling the text of the element that has focus.

Consider: You can limit the number of lines that a text element is permitted to use, even if the element requests TEXT_WRAP_ON. For example, you could decide that an element can use at most five lines. (Choose the actual number based on the size of your display.) If an element exceeds your limit, consider handling the contents in the same way that you handle elements with TEXT_WRAP_OFF.

Application Developers

Recommend: Use TEXT_WRAP_DEFAULT whenever possible so that the implementation can display your list elements in a way that meets the expectations of device users.

Consider: Use TEXT_WRAP_OFF to enable users to easily scan list elements with contents that are not under your control, such as a list of email subject lines.

5.2 Exclusive-Choice Lists

An exclusive-choice list is a screen of choices that always has one, and only one, element selected.

Application Developers

Strongly Recommend: The minimum size of an exclusive-choice list is two elements.

5.2.1 Selection in an Exclusive-Choice List

A selection makes a highlighted item become On (selected) and any previously selected element become Off (not selected).

MIDP Implementors

Strongly Recommend: Make sure an exclusive-choice list always has an element selected. Situations where the list will not have an element selected include when the application adds the first element to the list, provides all the list elements to the list constructor, or deletes the selected element. At these times, choose an element and select it. Do not display the list with no element selected.

Application Developers

Strongly Recommend: To have a particular element selected, set the selection explicitly, preferably before the list screen is visible. For example, set the selection immediately after creating the exclusive-choice list or just before deleting the currently selected element.

5.2.2 Abstract Commands on Exclusive-Choice List Screens

Application Developers

Strongly Recommend: Give exclusive-choice screens at least one abstract command. As shown in the left screen of Figure 5.6, an exclusive-choice screen needs an abstract command to handle the user's selection and move the user to another screen in the application.

Consider: Give exclusive-choice screens more than one abstract command so that users can either make a selection or move to another screen without making a choice. This applies the design consideration, "Make Everything Interruptible" on page 13.

For example, the right screen of Figure 5.6 shows a screen with two abstract commands: one is type Screen (labeled Save) and the other is type Back (labeled Back). (See "Types of Abstract Commands" on page 166 for more information.)

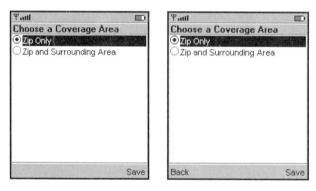

Figure 5.6 Exclusive-Choice Lists

The abstract command with the Save label sets the coverage area to the chosen value and moves the user to another screen in the application. The abstract command with the Back label returns the user to the previous screen. If the screen contained only the abstract command labeled Save, users would be forced to choose a setting in order to move to another screen.

The screen could have abstract commands for other tasks too.

5.2.3   Exclusive-Choice List Alternatives

Application Developers

> *Consider*: To enable users to choose among options on a form, use a choice group instead of an exclusive-choice list. See "Choice Groups" on page 116 for more information.

> *Consider*: Use an implicit list instead of an exclusive-choice list if you want a screen that operates like a menu. See "Implicit Lists" on page 48 for more information.

5.3   Multiple-Choice Lists

A multiple-choice list allows users to select zero or more elements. Each element in a multiple-choice list has two selection states: On (selected) or Off (not selected). If a user selects a multiple-choice element in the Off state, it becomes On; if the element is in the On state, it becomes Off.

Application Developers

> *Strongly Recommend*: The minimum size of a multiple-choice list is one element.

> *Consider*: Use a multiple-choice list with a single element to enable the user to toggle a state. For example, it could enable users to choose whether to hide or show part of the application. The multiple-choice element can be Off or On, indicating the desired state.

> *Strongly Recommend*: A multiple-choice screen must have at least one abstract command to handle the user's selections and move the user to another screen. (Follow the same rules as for "Exclusive-Choice Lists" on page 45.)

Recommend: Give multiple-choice screens more than one abstract command so that users can either make a selection or move to another screen without making a choice. This applies the design consideration, "Make Everything Interruptible" on page 13.

The multiple-choice lists could also have abstract commands for other tasks.

5.4   Implicit Lists

An implicit list has a default action associated with it. An implicit list enables a user to select one element and to perform its associated (*implied*) action on the selection.

Application Developers

Strongly Recommend: The minimum size of an implicit list is two elements.

Strongly Recommend: Make the implied action the primary task that you expect the user to accomplish with the screen. For example, a mail application might present a list of messages as an implicit list. The user could read the message, delete it, or file it in a different mailbox. The primary task, reading the message, should be the implied action.

Implicit lists have a default select command, SELECT_COMMAND, provided by the MIDP implementation. An application developer can associate the implied action with SELECT_COMMAND, but the user will be given only a neutral label, or no label, for the action. Figure 5.7 shows a list that uses the default SELECT_COMMAND. To choose an element and execute the implied action, the user must press the Select button. The implied action has no command label associated with a soft button.

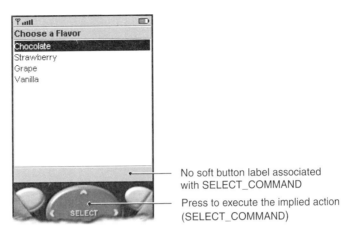

Figure 5.7 Implicit List with Only the Default SELECT_COMMAND

Recommend: Replacing SELECT_COMMAND with an abstract command allows you to provide a meaningful label to help direct users. The abstract command should be of type ITEM (the Select button will still signal your application that a SELECT_COMMAND has taken place). Figure 5.8 shows an abstract command (labeled Choose) provided by an application for the SELECT_COMMAND.

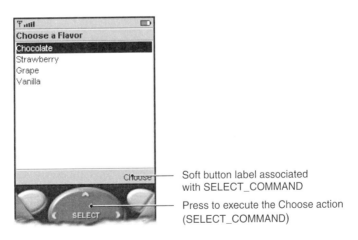

Figure 5.8 Implicit List with an Abstract Command for SELECT_COMMAND

An implicit-list screen can have abstract commands in addition to its implied action.

Application Developers

Consider: Give implicit-list screens an abstract command that enables users to move to another screen without acting on a choice. Provide this abstract command in addition to an implied action. This applies the design consideration, "Make Everything Interruptible" on page 13.

Figure 5.9 shows an implicit list with an abstract command that enables the user to move to another screen without making a choice.

Figure 5.9   Implicit List with an Abstract Command and an Implied Action

An implicit-list screen could also have abstract commands for other tasks. For example, SmartTicket has an implicit list that shows the available movies in the user's viewing area. The list's implied action could be to choose the selected movie. In addition, the screen could have abstract commands associated with it that allow the user to see a poster for the movie or return to the previous screen. Figure 5.10 shows what this screen could look like.

MIDP Implementors

Strongly Recommend: Do not allow users to invoke the Select command if there are no elements in the list. If there are no elements, disable the Select command and remove it from any soft button or menu.

Figure 5.10 SmartTicket's Implicit List with Additional Abstract Commands

CHAPTER 6

Text

$\mathbf{T}$EXT boxes are screens that can display one or more lines of text that the application usually allows the user to edit. Application developers can use text boxes to get input from the user or to show a screen of text; MIDP implementors can use them as editors for *text fields*. (A text field is similar to a text box, but is an item on a form. See Chapter 8 for information.) Figure 6.1 shows a text box on a mobile phone.

Figure 6.1   Text Box on a Mobile Phone

Application Developer Responsibilities	**MIDP Implementor Responsibilities**

• Abstract commands for the screen
• Any constraints and modifiers
• Any initial text
• Requested maximum number of characters (If greater than limit imposed by the MIDP implementor, the MIDP implementor's limit is used.)
	• Initial position of the caret
	• Largest possible size of a text box
	• How to scroll through a text box
	• Which input modes to support
	• Meaning of the constraints and modifiers
	• Mask character for the PASSWORD modifier
	• Whether to support cut, copy, and paste
	• Indication that a text box is not editable
	• If the text box is an editor for a text field:
	  - Title of the text box
	  - How to indicate editing is done
	  - How to leave without changing text

This chapter covers *constraints*, *modifiers*, and *input modes* before providing recommendations for text boxes. Constraints and modifiers are constants that enable an application developer to tailor a text box or text field for a specific task. Constraints are restrictive values; for example, one constraint limits input to numbers. Modifiers can be combined with each other or with a constraint to further affect the text box or field's behavior; for example, one modifier masks the user's input. An input mode is a setting that can make it easier for users to enter certain characters. (See *Programming Wireless Devices with the Java™ 2 Platform, Micro Edition* [17] for information on constraints, modifiers, input modes, and the TextBox API.)

6.1   Constraints

Applications can tailor the behavior of text boxes and text fields, and possibly the keyboard mappings of the device, by using the constants covered in this section. Applications can use one constraint per text box or text field.

Application Developers

Recommend: Use constraints. The implementation may be able to use them to limit the user's input and decrease user error.

6.1.1   The ANY Constraint

The ANY constraint permits the user to enter any character on the device. The characters available are device-dependent.

MIDP Implementors

Strongly Recommend: Your device must support, at a minimum, the characters in the ITU-T keypad (0-9, *, #). If your device does not have a keypad, give the user some other method of entering these characters. (For example, users of Palm OS devices could enter these characters using graffiti.)

6.1.2 The NUMERIC Constraint

The NUMERIC constraint limits the user to providing integer values, with an optional minus sign (-) to indicate that the integer is negative. Figure 6.2 shows a text field with a numeric constraint.

Figure 6.2 Text Field with a NUMERIC Constraint

MIDP Implementors

Strongly Recommend: Determine the mechanism for changing the sign of the value in the NUMERIC text box or field. For example, the MIDP Reference Implementation uses the star key (∗) to toggle the minus sign.

Strongly Recommend: You must ensure that the text box or text field is empty, or its value is an integer. You must not permit the user to enter any letters or other characters into a text box or field with a NUMERIC constraint.

Application Developers

Strongly Recommend: When you assign a maximum size (maximum number of characters) to a text box with a numeric constraint, remember to allow space for the minus sign if the user might enter a negative number. Users cannot enter negative numbers into text boxes that have a maximum size of one.

6.1.3   The DECIMAL Constraint

The DECIMAL constraint limits the user to providing only numeric values, with optional decimal fractions. For example, the following are legal values: -123, 0.123, and .5. Figure 6.3 shows a text field with a DECIMAL constraint.

Figure 6.3   Text Field with a DECIMAL Constraint

MIDP Implementors

    Strongly Recommend: You must ensure that a text box or field is either empty or that its value is a real number. You must not permit the user to enter any illegal characters into a text box or field with a DECIMAL constraint.

    Strongly Recommend: If the real number has a fractional part, it is separated from the integer part by a separator character that can vary depending on your implementation. The displayed character is typically a period (.) or comma (,) or some other character depending on the locale. Regardless of the character shown to the user, the actual value provided to the application must use the period (.) as the separator.

Application Developers

Strongly Recommend: Your MIDlet is responsible for parsing the string value of the text box into a numeric value suitable for computation.

Strongly Recommend: When you assign a maximum size to a text box with a DECIMAL constraint, remember to allow space for the sign and the fraction separator.

6.1.4   The PHONENUMBER Constraint

The PHONENUMBER constraint hints to the MIDP implementor that the user will be entering a phone number.

MIDP Implementors

Strongly Recommend: Determine whether the PHONENUMBER constraint limits the characters that the user can enter, the formatting of the value entered, or both.

Consider: Present the phone number (the contents of the text field) in a way that is readable by users. For example, although the content of the text field might be 4085551212, you could display it more readably as 408.555.1212 or (408) 555-1212.

Strongly Recommend: If you present the phone number to the user with additional characters, such as spaces, do not provide those extra characters to the application.

6.1.5   The EMAIL Constraint

The EMAIL constraint hints to the MIDP implementor that the user will be entering an email address.

MIDP Implementors

Strongly Recommend: Determine whether the EMAIL constraint limits the characters that the user can enter. For example, you might decrease user error by not allowing users to enter characters that are commonly invalid, such as slash (/), comma (,), colon (:), or semicolon (;).

Strongly Recommend: Do not capitalize the characters in a text box with an EMAIL constraint.

Application Developers

Strongly Recommend: Have your MIDlet check the contents of the text field if it requires a properly formatted email address. The application must validate the user's input because the MIDP specification does not require the device to do so.

6.1.6   The URL Constraint

The URL constraint hints to the MIDP implementor that the user will be entering a URL.

MIDP Implementors

Strongly Recommend: Determine whether the URL constraint limits the characters that the user can enter. For example, the valid characters in a domain name are letters, numbers and hyphens (-).

Strongly Recommend: Do not capitalize the characters in a text box with a URL constraint.

Application Developers

Strongly Recommend: Have your MIDlet check the contents of the text field if it requires a properly formed URL. The application must validate the user's input because the MIDP specification does not require the device to do so.

6.2   Modifiers

Application developers can also use modifiers to further affect the behavior of a text box or text field. Unlike a constraint, a modifier doesn't restrict the data that users can enter. Instead, modifiers can affect the way the device displays the data, the way the user enters or edits the data, and possibly the way the device is permitted to handle the data.

Application developers can use one or more modifiers with a constraint. For example, they can have the MIDP implementation use a mask character so that the contents of the text box or text field are not visible. This is commonly done when an application requests that the user enter a password or personal identification number (PIN). The contents of the text box or text field are not affected, only the display.

6.2.1   The INITIAL_CAPS_ Modifiers

The INITIAL_CAPS_SENTENCE modifier requests that during text editing the device capitalize the initial letter of each sentence. The INITIAL_CAPS_WORD modifier requests that during text editing the initial letter of each word be capitalized. Note that this modifier *does* affect the value stored in the text field: the text is stored with the capitalization. Figure 6.4 shows how text in text boxes with these modifiers could look.

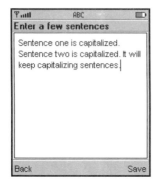

Figure 6.4 Sentence Capitalization and Word Capitalization Modifiers

Application Developers

 Recommend: Don't specify these modifiers in text boxes with an EMAIL or a URL constraint. It is not an error if you do, but they could make the value of the text box unusable. For example, case is important in some URLs—if the case is incorrect the URL will fail.

 Strongly Recommend: Don't specify both the INITIAL_CAPS_SENTENCE and INITIAL_CAPS_WORD modifiers in a single text box or field. Use one modifier or the other.

MIDP Implementors

 Strongly Recommend: Comply with the INITIAL_CAPS_SENTENCE and INITIAL_CAPS_WORD modifiers if automatic capitalization is appropriate and your character set has the notion of upper-case and lower-case letters.

 Strongly Recommend: If the application specifies both modifiers (INITIAL_CAPS_SENTENCE and INITIAL_CAPS_WORD) use the behavior of INITIAL_CAPS_WORD.

6.2.2   The `NON_PREDICTIVE` Modifier

The `NON_PREDICTIVE` modifier indicates that the text does not consist of words that are likely to be found in dictionaries typically used by predictive text-input schemes.

Application Developers

> *Consider*: Use this modifier in a text box that has a `URL`, `EMAIL`, `NUMERIC`, or `DECIMAL` constraint. Email addresses and domain names are not typical words, so turning off predictive text input would keep the device from distracting the user by unnecessarily offering suggestions. Similarly, predictive text-input systems are not useful when the user is entering numbers.

MIDP Implementors

> *Strongly Recommend*: If the application specifies the `NON_PREDICTIVE` modifier, allow users to enter one character at a time without any predictive input facilities. If the application does not specify this modifier, and your device has predictive input facilities, you can use them to help the user enter data.

6.2.3   The `PASSWORD` Modifier

The `PASSWORD` modifier indicates that the text is confidential data that should be obscured whenever possible. Figure 6.5 shows how this modifier could look.

Figure 6.5 `PASSWORD` Modifier

Application Developers

 Recommend: Use the PASSWORD modifier for text boxes and text fields that hold confidential information such as passwords or PINs.

 Recommend: Use the PASSWORD modifier with only the ANY and NUMERIC constraints. The MIDP specification does not limit the use of the PASSWORD modifier; however, using it with constraints other than ANY and NUMERIC, does not make sense.

MIDP Implementors

 Strongly Recommend: Choose which character to use as the masking character. The star (✳) is commonly used; it is shown in Figure 6.5.

Some devices do not immediately mask characters, so that users can see whether the system has received the character they intended to enter. For example, the character might appear unmasked for a brief time, or until the user types another character. This helps to decrease user error.

 Strongly Recommend: Follow your device conventions for masking the characters entered into a text box or field with a PASSWORD constraint. The behavior of your MIDP implementation will be more predictable if it provides the same behavior as the rest of the device.

 Strongly Recommend: Do not allow cutting or copying of the contents of a text box or text field that uses the PASSWORD modifier. Allowing this could be a security problem because the text would appear unmasked if it were then pasted into a text box or field that did not have a PASSWORD modifier.

 Strongly Recommend: Never store the contents of the text box or text field with a PASSWORD modifier into a dictionary or table for use in predictive, auto-completing, or other accelerated input schemes.

6.2.4 The SENSITIVE Modifier

The SENSITIVE modifier is similar to the PASSWORD modifier, but the SENSITIVE modifier does not obscure the contents of a text field.

Application Developers

Recommend: Use the SENSITIVE modifier for text boxes and text fields that hold less confidential information, such as credit card numbers, which, although private, do not need to be obscured.

MIDP Implementors

Strongly Recommend: Never store the contents of the text box or text field using the SENSITIVE modifier into a dictionary or table for use in predictive, auto-completing, or other accelerated input schemes.

6.2.5 The UNEDITABLE Modifier

The UNEDITABLE modifier indicates that the user is not permitted to edit the contents of the text box or text field. Figure 6.6 shows an example of how this modifier could look.

Figure 6.6 UNEDITABLE Modifier

MIDP Implementors

Strongly Recommend: When an application uses the UNEDITABLE modifier, prevent the user from changing the text contents of this object.

Recommend: Provide a visual indication that the text contents cannot be edited. You can also provide audio feedback, such as a beep sound, when the user tries to change the text.

Recommend: If you indicate that the text's contents are uneditable by changing the color of the text, conduct usability testing to verify that the text is still readable.

6.3   Input Modes

Input modes enable applications to request that a MIDP implementation make it convenient for the user to enter certain characters. For example, an application may have a text field or text box that has a NUMERIC constraint. To make data entry more convenient, the application could also request an input mode that makes it easy for the user to enter numbers.

Each input mode has a name, which typically describes its character set. An application requests an input mode by name. For example, the application could request an input mode of IS_LATIN_DIGITS to make it more convenient for the user to enter a number.

MIDP Implementors

Strongly Recommend: Indicate the device's current text mode to the user. Figure 6.7 shows two text modes, one numeric and one alphabetic, and points out the device's text input mode indicators.

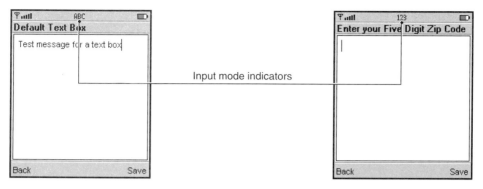

Figure 6.7 Input Mode Indicators

Possible input modes include *unicode character blocks,* as defined in the J2SE platform's `java.lang.Character.UnicodeBlock` class (such as `UCB_BENGALI`), and *input subsets* as defined in the J2SE platform's `java.awt.im.InputSubset` class (such as `IS_LATIN_DIGITS`). In addition, MIDP defines `MIDP_UPPERCASE_LATIN`, the subset of `IS_LATIN` that corresponds to uppercase Latin letters, and `MIDP_LOWERCASE_LATIN`, the subset of `IS_LATIN` that corresponds to lowercase Latin letters. Implementations can also create character subsets; see the *MIDP 2.0 Specification* [19] for more information.

 Strongly Recommend: Decide which input modes you will support, and publish them.

 Strongly Recommend: If you are unable to fulfill an application's input mode request, or the input mode is inconsistent with the text box or text field's current constraint setting, use a default input mode instead.

 Recommend: Change your default input mode according to the constraints of the text box or text field. For example, if the current constraint is `NUMERIC`, you could use a default input mode that makes it easy for the user to enter numerals, whereas if the constraint is `ANY`, your default input mode might allow the characters corresponding to the device's locale.

6.3.1   Requesting an Input Mode

Application Developers

Recommend: Request an input mode before the text box or text field is visible. If editing is already in progress, your request will not change the current input mode; it will take effect the next time the user initiates editing of this text object.

MIDP Implementors

Strongly Recommend: Use the requested input mode, if possible, whenever the user initiates the editing of a text box or text field, but allow the user to switch input modes at any time. Users must be permitted to enter any character that is allowed within the constraints of the text box or text field.

Strongly Recommend: If an application uses constraints and modifiers that conflict with its requested input mode, you must honor the constraints and modifiers. You are permitted to ignore the input mode in order to fulfill the requirements of the constraints and modifiers.

6.3.2   Providing Symbols Not on the Device

MIDP Implementors

Consider: Use a symbol table to show extra symbols that are not easily available from the device. If the device already has such a symbol table, consider giving the users access to it. Figure 6.8 shows a symbol table.

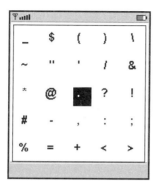

Figure 6.8 Symbol Table for Entering Characters

6.4   Handling Text Boxes

MIDP Implementors

Recommend: Wrap text on word boundaries, wrap words longer than one line on character boundaries, and honor white space. Text is most readable if it breaks on word boundaries. Further, it can be assumed that application developers and users include white space to improve readability, so applications will be more usable if the device honors this white space.

6.4.1   Updating Text, Constraints, and Modifiers

The application developer sets the initial text, along with any constraints and modifiers for the text box. The application developer can then insert, delete, and replace characters in the text box as needed. The application developer can also change the input constraints and modifiers of a text box as needed.

Application Developers

Consider: Do not try to change the contents of a text box or field while the user is editing it. If your change succeeds, it overwrites the user's work. It is also possible that your changes might be lost when the user indicates that the editing task is complete.

Application Developers, Continued

Consider: The up-to-date contents of a text box might not be visible while the user is editing it. The contents are updated when the application is notified that the user is done editing. (That is, when the user chooses an abstract command.)

Strongly Recommend: Do not change the constraint associated with a text box that the user is editing. Changing the constraint while the user is editing a text box makes the user's task more difficult.

6.4.2   Capacities of Text Boxes

The capacity of a text box is the maximum number of characters it can hold. The capacity of a text box does not affect its size. A text box is always a full-screen component.

MIDP Implementors

Recommend: Use the capacity of a text box to limit the user's input and decrease user error. For example, have the device beep and stop accepting additional input when the user reaches the capacity of the text box. (Because a text box is a type of screen, its capacity limits the legal number of input characters, not its size.)

Strongly Recommend: Set the maximum capacity (number of characters) of your text boxes, and publish this limit for your device so that the information is available to application developers.

Application Developers

Consider: Set text boxes to accept the largest number of characters you expect users to enter. If you know how much data users will put into a text box (for example, if you know it will hold a password between six and ten characters), you can make it more usable by setting it to accept the correct maximum number of characters. If you don't know how much data the user will enter, use the device's maximum value.

The MIDP implementation's limit is used if you request a higher capacity than it allows.

 Strongly Recommend: Check the maximum size of your text box or field after you create it to determine whether it has the capacity you requested. If it doesn't, your application should be able to work with the lower capacity.

CHAPTER 7

Forms and Form Layout

A FORM is a screen that can contain an arbitrary mixture of items: images, text fields, gauges, choice groups, and so on. (Note that the term *items* is used for components on a form, while *elements* is used for the choices in a list or choice group.) A form is intended to correspond to a task that the user can perform. Figure 7.1 shows a variety of form screens.

This chapter covers working with and laying out forms; Chapter 8 covers the items that can be in a form. It is best to read this chapter and Chapter 8 together.

 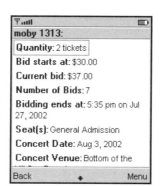 

Figure 7.1 Form Screens

Application Developer Responsibilities	MIDP Implementor Responsibilities
• Sequence of form items • Form item content • Preferred sizes of form items (optional) • At least one abstract command for the form	• Item minimum and maximum size • Layout of form items • Informing the application when the user updates a form item

7.1   Creating and Updating Forms

Keeping forms as short and as simple as possible makes them more usable. For example, users will need to do less traversal and scrolling to complete the form. Short, simple forms also use less memory and can improve performance. Laying out a form can be time consuming. If a device takes a long time to lay out and display a complex form, users will perceive it as a performance problem.

After creating a form, an application developer can change, add, or delete its items as needed. This process should not distract the user.

Application Developers

Strongly Recommend: Create forms that contain a small number of closely related items. The form should enable the user to perform one large task or two to three small tasks. The best guide for whether a particular form contains too many items is feedback from usability testing. The screens in Figure 7.1 each show a form that is designed for one task.

Recommend: Do not change a form's contents while the form is visible, unless it is in response to a user action, such as selecting an item. Making arbitrary changes while the user is interacting with the form can be disorienting, but users understand context-sensitive screens that change in response to their actions. Such forms have more predictable behavior and are faster for users to interact with.

Because an application is notified each time a user changes an item, an application developer could create content-sensitive forms that change their contents as a result of user actions. For example, the form shown in Figure 7.2 contains a custom item (it looks like a choice group with a single element). The item initially displays Select Theater. If the user selects a theater, the form changes to reveal additional items. If the user does not select a theater, the form's content is not changed.

Figure 7.2 Context-Sensitive Form

7.2   Form Layout Policy

The *MIDP 2.0 Specification* [19] provides rules for form layout. For example, it states that forms are organized in rows, and that each row is the same width, generally the width of the screen. (Forms are not expected to scroll horizontally. Devices are typically vertically oriented, and horizontal scrolling can be more confusing to users of small devices. However, horizontal scrolling is not prohibited.)

Working within the rules of the *MIDP 2.0 Specification*, MIDP implementors control the layout of forms on their devices. It is possible that different devices will lay out forms differently. Factors that affect form layout include the placement of item labels, the sizes of the items, the layout directives requested by the application, and so on.

Application developers use sizes, layout directives, and new lines to control the layout of the items on a form.

MIDP Implementors

 Recommend: Have a consistent, predictable layout policy that conforms to the *MIDP 2.0 Specification*, and publish the policy for developers.

7.2.1   Label Sizes

MIDP implementors decide how much space to give a label on their device. For example, some might decide that a label can be at most two lines long. Some might restrict a label to a single line. If a label is too long for a device, the MIDP implementor might have to clip the label.

MIDP Implementors

 Strongly Recommend: Determine and publish the maximum size label your forms can accommodate.

 Strongly Recommend: Coordinate label size with the minimum and default preferred sizes of your form items. In some cases, label size is included in the size of the item. See "Item Sizes" on page 76 for more information.

 Strongly Recommend: If you must clip labels due to device or maximum size restrictions, indicate to the user that the label has been shortened. A common way to indicate clipping is by using an ellipsis.

 Recommend: If you allow multiline labels, wrap text on word boundaries, wrap words longer than one line on character boundaries, and honor white space.

Text is most readable if it breaks on word boundaries. For example, users find titles such as the one in Figure 7.3, which do not wrap on word boundaries, much harder to read. Application developers can use white space to improve readability; applications will be more usable if the device honors this white space.

Figure 7.3 Not Recommended: Label Does Not Wrap on Word Boundaries

7.2.2   Label Visibility

It should be easy for users to associate a label with its item, because labels can act as prompts or headings for their items. For the same reason, it should be easy for a user to distinguish an item's label from its content.

MIDP Implementors

 Strongly Recommend: Keep a label near its component, either in the same row as the item or directly above it.

 Strongly Recommend: Coordinate the placement of the item label with the language of the device. For example, if your device can use a language that reads right to left or a language that reads left to right, position the label to accommodate the language the device is using.

 Recommend: Keep an item's label visible when its item is visible, even when you are scrolling the screen. (See "Scrolling" on page 84 for more information.)

 Strongly Recommend: Differentiate a label from its item by using techniques, such as putting the label on a line by itself; ending the label with a special character, such as a colon (:); or using a different font for the label.

Figure 7.4 shows a MIDP implementation that starts each label on a new line, places it flush left, just above its item's content, and uses a bold font.

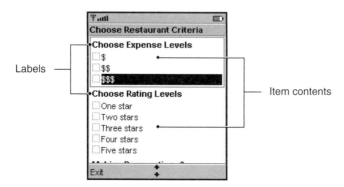

Figure 7.4 Differentiating Labels and Their Items on a Mobile Phone

7.2.3   Item Sizes

Items have a *minimum* size, a *preferred* size, and a *maximum* size. The MIDP implementor sets the minimum and maximum sizes. The preferred size (height, width, or both) can be set by the application developer.

An item's size refers only to the space that is significant to laying out the form. For example, if the MIDP implementation places item labels in a margin area reserved exclusively for labels, the space occupied by the label would not be considered part of the item's size. However, if item labels do not have a dedicated area, and other items have to move (in order to make room for the labels), then the space occupied by the labels is counted as part of the item's size.

MIDP Implementors

Recommend: Determine whether the label will be included in the item's size, and publish your decision for developers.

Strongly Recommend: Publish your minimum and maximum sizes for developers. You should also have a default preferred size that is known to developers.

The minimum size of a form item is the smallest size at which it can function and display its contents (though perhaps not optimally) on your device.

 Recommend: When you determine the minimum size of an item, consider issues such as choice-group elements, which must display some of their text to be usable.

 Strongly Recommend: Ensure that form items are usable at your minimum sizes.

The maximum size is the largest size that the device allows. The maximum width is typically based on the available screen width, fonts being used, and so on.

 Recommend: Determine the maximum height of an item based on the display height and the nature of the item. For example, a choice group that is longer than one screen will probably still be usable, but the same is not true for a gauge.

The preferred size is the smallest size at which no information is clipped and text wrapping (if any) is kept to a tolerable minimum. When an application sets a preferred height or width, it is called *locking* that value.

Application Developers

 Strongly Recommend: If you want an item to have a particular size, set its preferred size. The MIDP implementation will use your preferred size instead of its preferred or minimum size if possible. For example, if you do not want a picture to be clipped on the left or right, you could set the preferred width of the graphic item to the width of the image.

 Recommend: Allow the device to set the preferred height and width of items containing text, since you cannot know exactly what fonts it will be using.

MIDP Implementors

Strongly Recommend: If an application locks both the preferred width and height, truncate or pad the item as necessary to honor the request. If you cannot honor the request because of device restrictions, you may disregard the requested value and instead use your minimum or maximum value. If the locked size is smaller than your minimum size, use your minimum; if the locked size is larger than your maximum size, use your maximum.

Strongly Recommend: For items containing text, wrap the text to the specified width, and, if you must clip, do so only at the end of the text. (As with other text, if you must clip, give users a visual indication, such as an ellipsis.)

7.2.4   Item Padding

In addition to the size of an item, a MIDP implementation must account for item padding when it lays out a form. Items are typically padded so that there is some vertical and horizontal space between them. It not only makes the display easier to read, but also provides room for any traversal highlight. (See "Traversal and Selection Highlighting" on page 85 for more information.) When present, the padding is used for all items, independent of whether an item is displayed using its minimum or its preferred size.

MIDP Implementors

Strongly Recommend: Determine the amount of padding that you will use. Ensure that the additional space is enough to accommodate traversal highlighting, if your device uses it.

7.2.5   Layout Directives

Layout directives are constants that inform the MIDP implementation about the way the application developer wants the item to be placed in the form.

The LAYOUT_DEFAULT directive gives the MIDP implementation permission to lay out the item in whatever way is likely to be best for the device.

Application Developers

 Recommend: Use the LAYOUT_DEFAULT directive if you do not have any requirements for the way the form should be presented to the user.

The LAYOUT_2 directive has the MIDP implementation use the layout rules specified in the *MIDP 2.0 Specification* [19]. If this directive is not present, the MIDP implementation uses the layout rules specified in the *MIDP 1.0 Specification* [19]. The directive affects the handling of string and image items, as well as the placement of interactive items.

The *MIDP 1.0 Specification* requires string and image items that have labels to start a new row, while the *MIDP 2.0 Specification* does not. Similarly, the *MIDP 1.0 Specification* requires that an interactive item (such as a text field or an interactive gauge) start a new row, but this is not required by the *MIDP 2.0 Specification*. The LAYOUT_2 directive, therefore, can allow forms to be packed more tightly because string, image, and interactive items with the directive are permitted to share rows with other items.

Consider: If you want a string with a label, an image item with a label, or an interactive item to be on its own row, do not provide the LAYOUT_2 directive. On the other hand, if the item could share a row with surrounding items and still be understandable, use the LAYOUT_2 directive.

Consider: Many MIDP devices have relatively narrow screens. Even if you specify the LAYOUT_2 directive, the items may be on separate lines.

MIDP Implementors

Consider: An item with a LAYOUT_2 directive is permitted to share a row with other items, but it is not required to. Lay out the form in a way that is consistent with the native applications on your device.

The directives LAYOUT_SHRINK, LAYOUT_VSHRINK, LAYOUT_EXPAND, and LAYOUT_VEXPAND interact with item sizes. They inform the MIDP implementation that it can shrink or expand the item, as necessary, to lay out the form.

Application Developers

> *Consider*: Use the LAYOUT_SHRINK and LAYOUT_VSHRINK directives if the MIDP implementation can decrease the item to its minimum width or height, respectively. For example, if you put a text field with a PASSWORD modifier on a form, you might not mind if it were shown at its minimum size: the contents of the item would be obscured anyway.

> *Consider*: Use the LAYOUT_EXPAND, and LAYOUT_VEXPAND directives if the MIDP implementation can increase the item's width or height, respectively, to fill the available space. For example, if the most important item on your form is a gauge, you might not mind if its size were increased. The larger size would just help to capture the user's attention.

Other layout directives affect how an item is placed in its row. The directives LAYOUT_LEFT, LAYOUT_RIGHT, and LAYOUT_CENTER affect horizontal placement. The directives that affect vertical placement of an item are LAYOUT_TOP, LAYOUT_BOTTOM, and LAYOUT_VCENTER.

> *Strongly Recommend*: Do not use more than one horizontal placement directive and one vertical placement directive for each item. The directives that affect horizontal placement are mutually exclusive, as are the directives that affect vertical placement.

MIDP Implementors

> *Strongly Recommend*: You can put items with different vertical placement directives on the same row. For example, one item can be aligned with the top of the row while another item in the row can be aligned with the bottom. You cannot put items with different horizontal placement directives on the same row, however. If two items have different horizontal placement directives, you must start a new row for the second item, even if it would fit on the previous line.

Figure 7.5 shows forms with different vertical placement directives (the items are on the same line) and different horizontal placement directives (the items are on different lines).

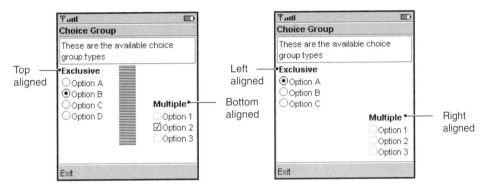

Figure 7.5 Vertical and Horizontal Placement Directives in a Form

Still other directives determine whether an item will start or end a row. The directive LAYOUT_NEWLINE_BEFORE ensures that an item will start a new row, while the directive LAYOUT_NEWLINE_AFTER ensures that an item will end a row. These directives cause only one row break, however. That is, if an item with a LAYOUT_NEWLINE_AFTER directive is followed by an item with a LAYOUT_NEWLINE_BEFORE directive, there will be only one row break.

7.2.6 New Lines in String Items

A string item can contain newline characters (\n) to request a new line. A MIDP implementation must provide one new row for each newline character in the string.

Application Developers

Recommend: If you want multiple row breaks in a form (that is, if you want empty rows), put multiple \n characters sequentially in string items instead of using layout directives. Figure 7.6 shows a form with the string item, "The first row\n\nThe third row."

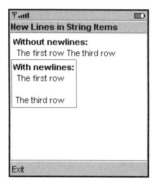

Figure 7.6 Effect of Multiple New Lines in a String Item

MIDP Implementors

Strongly Recommend: When you create empty rows because an application has used multiple sequential newline characters, make the height of each empty row the height of a line of text in the current font.

7.3   Traversing and Scrolling Forms

Users need a way to move through forms that are more than one screen long. Devices often use arrow keys to allow users to traverse or scroll (or both). Traversal moves the focus highlight up or down one item or item element at a time. Scrolling moves smoothly through a form, often approximately a screen at a time. Traversal can result in scrolling: If a user traverses to the end of the screen, a device might scroll a new screen of information into view. Scrolling, on the other hand, does not result in traversal and therefore does not change which item has focus.

MIDP Implementors

Strongly Recommend: If the user traverses to an item that is not visible, scroll the form to make it visible. Follow user focus so that the user's current item is always shown on the display.

Whether a device supports traversal, scrolling, or both, users need to know when a form is more than one screen long, and when they are at the top or bottom of a form. A scroll indicator is used for this purpose.

Strongly Recommend: Have the scroll indicator show users when they are at the top or bottom of the form. Turn off the up scroll indicator at the top of the form; turn off the down scroll indicator at the bottom of the form. Figure 7.7 shows the MIDP Reference Implementation, which uses both the up and down scroll indicators only when the user is not at the top or bottom of the form.

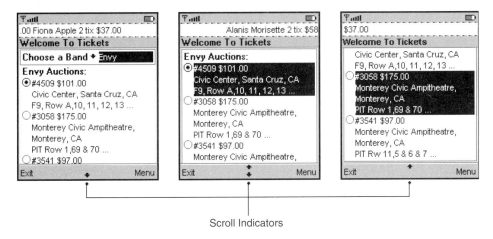

Scroll Indicators

Figure 7.7 Scroll Indicators at the Top, Middle, and Bottom of a Form

7.3.1 Traversal

How traversal operates on a form depends on what input mechanisms are available on it. If the device has only an Up and Down button, then traversal will move through the items on a form in the order they are presented. In some cases moving Down will actually move the traversal highlight to the right if that is where the next item is.

If a device has Up, Down, Left, and Right controls, then traversal can be two-dimensional. The user can press Down or Up to move to the next row and press Right or Left to move to the next item in a row.

Other devices might not support traversal. For example, a device with a touch screen might not have a way for users to move their focus one element at a time. It may give the user a way to scroll through the form, and expect the user to tap an element to give it focus.

MIDP Implementors

Strongly Recommend: If your device supports traversal, make sure that the user can traverse to all of the items on the form. There should be no traps that enable a user to traverse to, but not away from, an item.

In order to avoid traps, you must resolve the interaction between using keys to traverse and using them to edit items. For example, if you want to use the Left and Right arrow keys to edit the values on an interactive gauge, then you cannot use those keys to traverse into and out of the item. In that case, you could use only Up and Down to traverse into and out of gauges. In addition to gauges, exclusive- and multiple-choice groups, pop-up choice groups, and text fields require traversal solutions that are tuned to the input keys available on the device.

Recommend: Enable users to traverse to all of the items on a form using just one button so that they can use the form one-handed if necessary. For example, on a device with only Up and Down buttons, a user on the first item on a form should be able to press Down continuously to move from one item to the next to the end of the form. Pressing Right should work the same way on a device with Up, Down, Right, and Left buttons.

7.3.2   Scrolling

Consider: Use the device's volume key to scroll up and down if you want to support scrolling and no other button on the device is appropriate. This solution will be consistent with many device implementations of browsers.

The amount of the screen that scrolls at a time is device-dependent. Scrolling too far, though, can make it difficult for the user to know where they are on the form. They could become concerned that they have missed one or more items.

Recommend: Keep at least one line of context when scrolling a form. Keeping a line of context helps users to know that they have not scrolled further than they intended.

Recommend: When the user scrolls in a form, the top of the screen should display an entire item (as opposed to, for example, just the last line of a multiline element in a choice group). Note that an item includes any label associated with it. If an item is more than one screen in length, the top of the screen should display a full line of the item (as opposed to, for example, cutting off the tops of the letters). Once the item has been viewed, go to the next item.

7.4 Traversal and Selection Highlighting

A MIDP implementation shows users where they are in a form as they traverse through it by changing the appearance (*highlighting*) of the item that has focus. For example, as shown in Figure 7.8, the MIDP Reference Implementation uses a gray line.

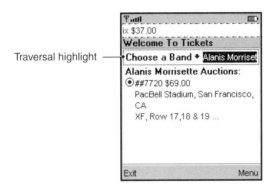

Figure 7.8 Traversal Highlight in the MIDP Reference Implementation

 Strongly Recommend: Use a traversal highlight only on interactive items. The MIDP Reference Implementation uses a traversal highlight for every item in a form. Figure 7.9 shows an example of this behavior. User feedback indicates that this is not always the best solution.

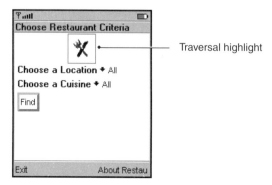

Figure 7.9 Not Recommended: Traversal Highlight on Noninteractive Item

In addition to the traversal highlight, the MIDP implementation can provide a *selection highlight*. This is useful within items, such as choice groups, to show users which element in the group would be selected if the user carried out the selection operation. (The mechanism for carrying out the selection is device-specific. In the MIDP Reference Implementation, the user would press the Select key.)

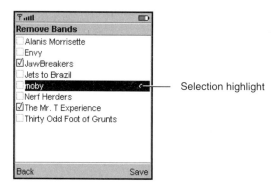

Figure 7.10 Selection Highlight

CHAPTER 8

Form Items

FORMS can contain one or more items. Some items are editable, such as text fields, and some are static, such as images. Application developers can give all items a label, a command, layout directives, and a preferred size. Because layout directives and sizes affect form layout, they are covered in Chapter 7. It is best to read this chapter and Chapter 7 together.

8.1   Labels

All items can have a label, which is a string associated with the item. Figure 8.1 shows an item with a label.

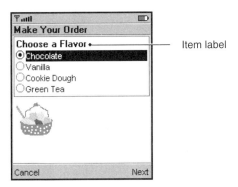

Item label

Figure 8.1   Item Label on a Form

Application Developer Responsibilities	MIDP Implementor Responsibilities
• Any label text	• Text-display policy (wrapped or clipped) • Placement in relation to item content • Item placement if label is not present • Font and color (if different from item font) • Visibility as the user scrolls through a form • Whether to use as the title of the editing screen for items edited off the form • Maximum size of a label

For information on laying out labels on a form, see "Label Sizes" on page 73. For information on labels and how to use them when a user edits an item off the form, see "System-Generated Screens" on page 36.

Application Developers

 Strongly Recommend: Provide labels that act as a prompt or provide instructions to the user for all interactive items.

 Recommend: Keep your labels short and to the point to conserve space on small displays. Limit their length to two lines on a small screen (test the application on a device with a small screen, such as one with dimensions of 96-by-54 pixels). Use wording that makes sense, even if it is shortened, to help keep your application usable even if its labels must be clipped.

Consider: You can change an item label as needed. Try to do it only when the form is not visible or in response to a user action. Arbitrary changes to visible screens are confusing to users.

8.2   Item-Specific Abstract Commands

An item-specific abstract command is an action that an application developer assigns to an item. In other words, it is an abstract command that an application developer associates with a form item instead of with the form screen. (See Chapter 12 for information on commands.)

A form item can have one or more commands associated with it. For string and image items, an item-specific abstract command helps to change its appearance from plain to a button or a hyperlink. See "Buttons and Hyperlinks" on page 97 for more information on how commands help to change the appearance of some form items.

Application Developers

 Strongly Recommend: Make the commands associated with form items be of type ITEM. Assign priorities if the item has more than one item-specific command. (See "Types of Abstract Commands" on page 166 for more information.)

 Recommend: If you find that you are associating the same command with every item on a screen, associate the command with the screen itself instead of with the individual items. When you associate the command with the screen, it should still be of type ITEM so that the device implementation can order the commands properly.

MIDP Implementors

 Strongly Recommend: Treat commands associated with a form item as type ITEM, no matter what type the application developer has specified. Give item-specific abstract commands higher precedence than ITEM commands associated with the screen.

 Strongly Recommend: If an item has multiple commands associated with it, make the commands available in the same way as commands associated with the screen. (See "Implementing Abstract Commands" on page 174 for more information.) Figure 8.2 shows item-specific abstract commands on a system menu with other abstract commands.

 Strongly Recommend: Make item-specific abstract commands available to the user only when the item has focus. Figure 8.2 shows this behavior in the MIDP Reference Implementation. The system menu changes as the focus changes. The items that have focus in the first and third screen shots have item-specific commands; the item in the second screen shot does not.

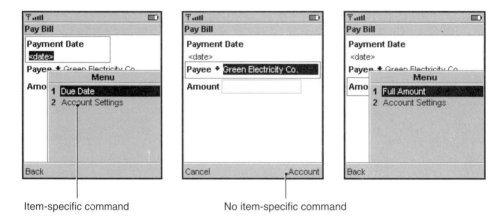

Item-specific command   No item-specific command

Figure 8.2   Item Commands

A form item can have a special item-specific abstract commands, called a *default command*. A default command is an item-specific abstract command that the MIDP implementation can bind to a device-specific selection gesture. If present, it should represent the action that the user would most strongly associate with the item. For example, consider a form item that is an audio player. Its most likely action would be Play; this action would map well to a device-specific selection gesture such as a Select key.

Application Developers

Strongly Recommend: If you have an action that a user would strongly associate with a particular item, make it the item's default command.

Consider: Because the default command's label could be invisible on some devices, make sure a default command leads to an action that the user would strongly associate with that item. For example, if the MIDP implementation binds the default command only to the device's Select key, the user would not see your label.

MIDP Implementors

Strongly Recommend: If an item has a default command, bind that command to a special user gesture that is appropriate to your device. For example, if your device has a Select key, you could bind the default command to that key. Similarly, if your device has touch input, tapping the item might invoke the item's default command.

Note that binding an item's default command to a user gesture, such as a Select key, might not be appropriate for some types of form items. For example, the default selection gesture, when applied to a pop-up choice group, typically makes the choice group's elements appear. Since the user already expects that behavior, the device should not use the Select key for the default command in this case.

Strongly Recommend: If there are circumstances under which you would not use the label of an item's default command (for example, if you bind the command only to the Select key), publish the information for application developers.

Strongly Recommend: Make the default command available in the same way you make abstract commands available to the user. (Give the default command the highest precedence within the commands of type ITEM.) For example, you might add the default item-specific command to a system menu. Do this in addition to binding the command to a special user gesture.

If you always make default item-specific commands available in the same way that other commands are available, users always know how to find the command. It would be confusing to have to use different methods on different form items to choose the default command.

8.3   Images

A form can contain one or more image items, each of which can contain a reference to an image. Figure 8.3 shows an image item.

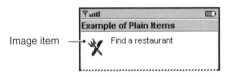

Figure 8.3   An Image Item on a Form

Application Developer Responsibilities	MIDP Implementor Responsibilities
• An immutable image • Any alternate text • Any label text • Any layout hints • Any item-specific abstract commands • Any appearance mode • Any item-specific abstract commands	• Any size or color constraints • Support for images in PNG format • Image-handling policy (clipping or skipping oversized images) • Alternate text support • Transparency support

Application Developers

Recommend: Provide high-contrast images because devices might not have high-quality color screens, and they are used in high-glare environments.

Consider: You can change, add, or remove an image from a form as needed. Try to do it only when the form is not visible, or in response to a user action. Arbitrary changes to visible screens are confusing.

Consider: You can make an image item interactive by adding an item-specific abstract command to it. In addition, you can change the appearance of the interactive image item so that it looks like a button or a hyperlink. See "Buttons and Hyperlinks" on page 97 for more information.

8.3.1 Image Format

MIDP implementations must support PNG (portable network graphics) 1.0 images, as specified in the W3C recommendation [24]. More information is available from RFC 2083 [25].

MIDP Implementors

> *Consider*: You can support other image formats in addition to supporting PNG. If you do support other image formats, publish this information for application developers.

Application Developers

> *Strongly Recommend*: For your MIDlet to run on as many devices as possible, provide PNG images. All MIDP devices support PNG graphics.

8.3.2 Transparency

Although all images are rectangular, transparency can enable them to appear to be different shapes. For example, an image of a ball can appear to be round.

There are two types of transparency: full and partial. When an image uses *full transparency*, its pixels are either transparent or opaque. The device uses the background color for the transparent pixels. For *partial transparency*, a pixel can be fully transparent, opaque, or some value in between.

MIDP Implementors

> *Consider*: You must support full transparency, but you are not required to support partial transparency. If you want to support partial transparency, your implementation will have to blend the partially transparent pixel with another pixel. If the pixel you blend against is the background pixel, it is called *full alpha blending*. Full alpha blending can be very resource intensive. It is not required by the *MIDP 2.0 Specification* [19], even for MIDP implementations that support partial transparency.

MIDP Implementors, Continued

Consider: If full alpha blending slows your implementation, try blending against a single color instead. The *MIDP 2.0 Specification* [19] does not require you to check the background color as part of your support for partial transparency.

8.3.3   Image Color and File Size Considerations

Small devices have limited resources, and image files can be large. This section offers some advice that will help reduce the file size of your images. Image files that use less storage space conserve device resources and enable MIDlets to start faster. In addition, they could save the user money: smaller MIDlet suites take less time to download.

Application Developers

Consider: When you create images for an application, consider saving them with only the colors they need. The fewer colors an image contains, the smaller its file size.

Consider: Provide a color image that looks good in grayscale instead of providing both a color and a grayscale version of the same image. Providing a single image that can serve both purposes saves space. (You may also need to provide a black-and-white version of the image if your MIDlet might be run on a monochrome device.)

Consider: If you provide more than one version of an image (for example, one that is color and another that is black and white), check the device characteristics at runtime to determine which version to use. The `Display` class has methods that return information such as the number of colors the device supports. (See *Programming Wireless Devices with the Java™ 2 Platform, Micro Edition* [17] for more information.)

8.3.4 Alternate Text

Alternate text is text that the MIDP implementation displays if it cannot show an image. For example, some devices would display alternate text if the image is too large.

Application Developers

 Recommend: Provide alternate text either when you create the image-item instance, or afterwards, using the `setAltText` method of the `ImageItem` class.

8.4 Strings

String items are texts that are displayed on forms and cannot be edited by the user. They are useful for conveying information to the user. Figure 8.4 shows a string item on a form.

Figure 8.4 A String Item on a Form

Application Developer Responsibilities	MIDP Implementor Responsibilities
• String text • Any label text • Any layout directives • Any preferred size • Any appearance mode • Any font suggestion • Any appearance mode • Any item-specific abstract commands	• String font • Layout hint support • Text-display policy (wrapped or clipped) • Minimum and maximum size

Application Developers

Consider: You can add, change, or remove a string item, its attributes, or its label as needed. Try to do it only when the form is not visible or in response to a user action. Arbitrary changes to visible screens are confusing to users.

Consider: You can make a string item interactive by adding an item-specific abstract command. In addition, you can change the appearance of the interactive item so that it looks like a button or a hyperlink. (See "Buttons and Hyperlinks" on page 97 for more information.)

MIDP Implementors

 Recommend: Wrap text on word boundaries, wrap words longer than one line on character boundaries, and honor white space.

Text is most readable if it breaks on word boundaries. Application developers can use white space to improve readability; applications will be more usable if the device honors this white space.

 Strongly Recommend: Avoid clipping string items because the item content is likely to provide information that the user must see (as opposed to labels, which are typically less critical). If you must clip a string item due to device restrictions, indicate to the user that it has been shortened. A common way to indicate clipping is by using an ellipsis.

8.5   Buttons and Hyperlinks

Both string and image items have an appearance mode attribute. Table 8.1 shows the attribute values, along with screen shots and short explanations.

Table 8.1: Appearance Modes

Attribute Value	Screen Shot	Description
PLAIN	Example of Plain Items — Find a restaurant	Default mode, typically used for noninteractive display of textual or graphical material.
HYPERLINK	Example of Hyperlinks — Find a restaurant	Requests that the device display the item contents as if the item were a hyperlink in a browser.
BUTTON	Example of Buttons — Find a restaurant	Requests that the device display the item contents as if the item were a button.

MIDP Implementors

Strongly Recommend: Display the hyperlink and button appearance modes in a way that is consistent with their purposes. The appearance mode should be an indication to the user whether the item is interactive. If an application requests a button or hyperlink appearance mode, but does not assign a command to the item, display the item as though it had a PLAIN appearance mode.

8.5.1   Hyperlink Appearance Mode

The hyperlink appearance mode should be similar in use to a web link. It can take the user to a new screen in the same way, conceptually, that a web link takes the user to a new page. Unlike a web link, however, an item with a hyperlink cannot take the user outside the MIDlet.

Application Developers

 Strongly Recommend: Use hyperlink appearance mode when the item enables the user to get more information. The hyperlink would take the user to another screen in the MIDlet. For example, if a person is buying tickets for a concert, a hyperlink can be used to access related secondary information, such as a map of the venue.

 Recommend: An item with hyperlink appearance mode should have one or more item-specific abstract commands associated with it. Without at least one associated command, the item is not interactive and a device might not display the item as a hyperlink.

Usability studies showed that an underline is helpful to indicate a hyperlink state, but merely underlining a hyperlink was not enough to indicate to users that a hyperlink had focus. Without an additional focus indicator, the user may not know that the link is selectable.

MIDP Implementors

Consider: Use a highlighting method, such as reverse video, to indicate when a hyperlink has focus. Figure 8.5 shows two hyperlinks, one with reverse-video to indicate it has focus.

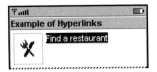

Figure 8.5 Hyperlink String When It Has Focus

8.5.2   Button Appearance Mode

The button appearance mode should be similar in use to a button on a web page: It should enable the user to carry out a command or operation. The button appearance mode should not take the place of abstract commands.

Application Developers

Strongly Recommend: Use a button appearance mode when the item enables a user to carry out a command or an operation.

Recommend: Give an item with a button appearance mode one item-specific abstract command, and make that command the item's default command. Without at least one associated command, the item is not interactive and a device might not display the item as a button. With more than one item-specific abstract command, the button will violate user expectations of being able to select it to take a particular action. They might not even realize that they should look to see what other item-specific commands are available.

Consider: Remember that in traversal-based devices, such as many mobile phones, users must navigate to a button before they can use it. If all of the fields preceding a button require a user's attention or interaction, users will not be inconvenienced by the navigation; a button could be appropriate. If, however, a button is at the end of a long form that includes optional items, traversing to the button could make the form seem cumbersome, and users could miss the button.

There are a few alternatives that application designers can consider instead of putting a button at the end of a long form. One alternative is to attach the command to the form itself. (See Chapter 12 for more information on commands associated with screens.) Attaching the command to the form places the command in a place that is always immediately accessible to the user. Figure 8.6 shows an example command, Find, attached to the form.

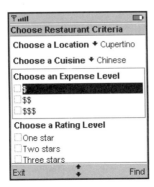

Figure 8.6   Form without a Button

Another alternative is to have two buttons on the form that perform the action. Place one button immediately after the required information, and the other after the optional information at the bottom of the form. Figure 8.7 shows an example of this type of form.

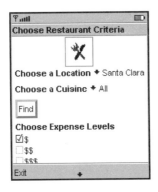 

Figure 8.7   Form with Two Buttons

Application Developers

Recommend: Do not use the appearance modes to create a button-based user interface. Instead, use abstract commands whenever possible. (See Chapter 12 for more information on abstract commands.)

There are a few reasons for this advice. One reason is that devices differ from one another in critical features, such as screen size. These differences make laying out the buttons in a way that is both portable and usable across devices very difficult.

Another reason is that MIDP is designed so that a device manufacturer can map abstract commands onto the device in a way that is expected by its users. This decreases the time required for the user to learn to use the MIDlet. Button-based user interfaces hamper usability by removing the device manufacturer's opportunity to unify the user experiences of MIDlets and native applications. When manufacturers are given this opportunity, users will find the device and all of its applications (MIDlets and native) both fast and predictable.

Finally, scrolling or traversing to a button is much slower than activating a soft key (a common method of making abstract commands available to users). Attaching abstract commands to a screen instead of creating a button-based user interface can make using the form less cumbersome.

MIDP Implementors

> *Consider*: A button needs two styles for focus highlighting, one to indicate a neutral state, and another to indicate when the button has focus. The MIDP Reference Implementation uses a 3-D style that looks like a raised button when it does not have focus, and a depressed button when it has focus. Figure 8.8 shows these button styles.

> *Consider*: Do usability testing to ensure your users can distinguish a button that is in a neutral state from one that has focus. For example, if users had problems distinguishing the focus state in the button graphics shown in Figure 8.8, you could add additional cues for the user, such as also displaying the depressed button in reverse video.

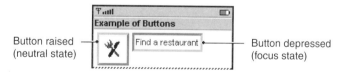

Figure 8.8 Neutral and Focus States of Button Items

8.6   Text Fields

Text fields are editable areas on a form that can display one or more lines of text. They can be used by application developers to get input from the user. Figure 8.9 shows a text field on a mobile phone. The text field, which has a PASSWORD modifier, is the box beside the item labeled Enter PIN.

Figure 8.9   Text Field on a Form

Application Developer Responsibilities	MIDP Implementor Responsibilities
• Any label text • Requested size, in characters, of text field • Any initial text • Any constraints • Any modifiers	• Initial size of the text field • Maximum size, in characters, of text fields • Stopping users input at text-field capacity • Initial position of the caret • Whether text is highlighted for overwriting when the user enters the field • Whether editing is in-place or off the form • Text-display policy (wrapped, clipped, or scroll-through) • Traversal method for moving through text • Constraint behavior • Mask character for PASSWORD modifier • Cut, copy, and paste support (optional)

Application Developers

> *Consider*: You can add, change, or remove the contents of a text field or its label as needed. Try to do it only when the form is not visible or in response to a user action. Arbitrary changes to visible screens are confusing to users.

8.6.1 Text Field Capacity

Text fields have capacities, which specify the maximum number of characters they can hold.

Application Developers

> *Consider*: Set text fields to accept an appropriate number of characters. If you know how much data users will put into a text field, you can make the text field more usable by setting it to accept the correct maximum number of characters. For example, if you have a text field that will hold a password between six and ten characters, set the text field capacity to ten.

If you don't know how many characters a user will be entering, enter the device's maximum number (this is available from the getMaxSize method). If you request a higher capacity than the MIDP implementation can provide, the MIDP implementation's capacity is used. If you are concerned, you can check the capacity of the text field, after your request, to see whether you were able to get the entire amount.

> *Recommend*: Allow the device to determine the physical size of the text field on the display. Do not set a preferred size yourself. (See "Item Sizes" on page 76 for more information.)

MIDP Implementors

> *Strongly Recommend*: Determine and publish the maximum number of characters that your text fields can hold.

Recommend: Use the capacity of a text field to limit the user's input and decrease user error. For example, have the device beep and stop accepting additional input when the user reaches the capacity of the text field.

 Recommend: Use the text field's capacity to determine the size to draw the text field on the form. For example, if a text field has a small capacity, you might draw it with only enough space to show the possible characters that it can accept.

Consider: If a text field's capacity is large enough that it can accept multiple lines of input, conserve screen real estate by showing space for only one line of text when the text field is empty. It is easier for the user to see and scroll through the form if the empty field is only one line in height.

8.6.2 Text Field Focus

The issues relating to text field focus include not only how to show that a text field has focus, but also to show whether a text field with focus can be edited on the form, whether a text field that has just gotten focus will have its text highlighted, and so on.

MIDP Implementors

 Strongly Recommend: Differentiate between a text field that has focus and one that does not. For example, you could make the outline of a text field that has focus black and put a cursor in the field. In contrast, you could make the outline of a text field that does not have focus a lighter gray line, and not put a cursor in the field. This strategy is shown in Figure 8.10.

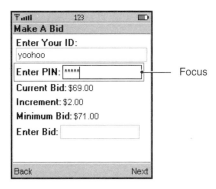

Figure 8.10 Showing Focus for Text Fields

 Strongly Recommend: Decide whether a text field is edited on the form or off the form in a text box, and publish your decision for application developers. (See Chapter 6 for more information on text boxes.)

 Strongly Recommend: If the text field will be edited on the form, determine whether you will highlight the contents of the text field for overwriting when the field gets focus. Make your MIDP implementation consistent with the behavior of the device.

 Strongly Recommend: If the text field will be edited off the form, the text field on the form should show its entire contents. This keeps the user from having to leave the form to see what is in the text field. If the capacity of the text field is large, the text field can be small when it does not have focus (for example, display a single line of text) but grow to capacity when it has focus.

 Strongly Recommend: When a text field is the first visible item on a form, put the focus on that field, show a caret, and be ready to accept input from the user as soon as the screen is displayed.

8.7   Dates and Times

A date field is an item that presents an editable date, time, or both to the user. All date fields are editable. Figure 8.11 shows a date field that presents a date and time to the user.

Figure 8.11 A Date Field on a Form

Application Developer Responsibilities	MIDP Implementor Responsibilities
• Any label text • Any initial value of the field • Type of date field to use (date, time, or both)	• Presentation of the date and time • Presentation of an uninitialized date field • How users enter and edit the date, time, or both

Application Developers

Consider: You can change the contents of a date field or its label as needed. Try to do it only when the form is not visible or in response to a user action. Arbitrary changes to visible screens are confusing to users.

MIDP Implementors

Consider: Determine whether you will have users edit the date and time values on the form, or on a separate screen. Figure 8.12 shows a date and a time ready for editing off the form.

Figure 8.12 Editing a Date Field on a Separate Screen

8.8   Gauges

A gauge is a visual display of a value. A gauge can be editable (an *interactive gauge*) or not editable (a *noninteractive gauge*). A typical use for an interactive gauge is enabling the user to set a volume level; a typical use for a noninteractive gauge is to give the user feedback on the application's progress through a long task. Figure 8.13 shows an interactive gauge on a mobile phone.

Figure 8.13 Gauge on a Mobile Phone

There are three types of noninteractive gauges: a *progress bar*, an *incremental gauge*, and a *continuous gauge*. A typical use of a progress bar is to show the user the device's progress through a file transfer when the file's size is known. It can show how far the task is from completing.

A typical use of an incremental gauge is to show the user the device's progress through a file transfer when the file's size is not known. The device can tell it is receiving data, so the gauge can provide feedback to indicate that the task is progressing, but it cannot tell the user how far it is from the end of the task.

A typical use of a continuous gauge is to let the user know the device is using the network to request information. The device cannot tell whether the server is making progress toward getting the requested information, nor can it tell when the requested information will arrive. It merely provides feedback that the application is still running and the device is not broken.

Application Developer Responsibilities	**MIDP Implementor Responsibilities**
• Which type of gauge to use • Any label text • Any initial value of the gauge • Maximum value of the gauge • Current value or state of the gauge	• Visual appearance of interactive and noninteractive gauges • Mapping the value of the gauge to the screen space available for the gauge • How users edit interactive gauge value • Informing the application when the user changes the value of an interactive gauge

MIDP Implementors

Recommend: Create different visual appearances for the different types of gauges so that users can easily see the purpose of the gauge. For example, they should be able to tell whether they can use a gauge to change a setting or only get to information from it. If they can only get information from it, they should also be able to tell which type of information it is imparting.

8.8.1   Interactive Gauges

An interactive gauge enables the user to set a value. For example, an application could use an interactive gauge to enable the user to enter a value that controls the pace of a game. An interactive gauge has a range of values from zero to an application-defined maximum value.

Application Developers

Strongly Recommend: Set a small maximum value in a gauge (at most, provide a range of a few dozen values). If the value is for an API that expects a broader range of values, map the gauge value onto the broader range.

For example, consider an API that controls a volume level by accepting a parameter expressed as a percentage (0 to 100) of maximum. Most devices don't have 100 distinct volume levels. It would be reasonable to use a gauge to represent a smaller range that is then mapped onto the 0 to 100 range expected by the API. To do this, the application would create a gauge with a maximum value of, for example, 20. It would then map this into the 0 to 100 range by computing (gauge-value * 5).

There are two reasons to keep the range of values small. First, it will help to keep the range of values closer to the number of distinct visual states possible on most devices. The closer these values are, the fewer values share the same visual representation. This will make your gauge appear to be more responsive.

Second, it will improve application usability. In many cases, the only means for the user to modify the value of an interactive gauge will be to press a button to increase or decrease the gauge's value by one. Keeping the range of values relatively small means that the user will probably have less work to do to change the value of the gauge.

MIDP Implementors

Consider: Use a visual representation for interactive gauges that distinguishes the smaller values from the larger values. For example, Figure 8.14 shows a gauge that has shorter bars on the left, representing smaller values, and longer bars on the right, representing higher values.

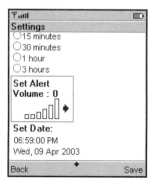

Figure 8.14 Interactive Gauge

MIDP Implementors, Continued

 Recommend: Show as fine-grained a display of values as possible. Interactive gauges that show more values provide users with more visual feedback about their value. Giving users as much feedback as possible allows them to feel more in control of the device.

 Strongly Recommend: Normalize the range of possible values for a gauge into a smaller set of values for display purposes. (Note that normalizing values for display does *not* change the actual value of the gauge.) For example, if your device can display 10 bars, and an application creates a gauge that has a maximum value of 99, show one bar for the values zero through nine, two bars for values 10 through 19, and so on.

 Strongly Recommend: Provide a way to change the value of a gauge quickly. For example, implement key-repeat for changing the gauge value. As another example, some devices have two types of scroll buttons: those for small increments and those for large increments. If your device is like this, you could use the scroll buttons for large increments to move in the increments spanned by a bar on your display.

Consider: Use a different visual state, instead of reverse video, to show that an interactive gauge has focus. Using reverse video to show that a gauge has focus can be confusing. Figure 8.15 shows an alternative to using reverse video for highlighting. It draws the unfilled bars with black lines when the gauge has focus and gray lines when it does not. (On black-and-white displays, it uses solid versus dotted lines.)

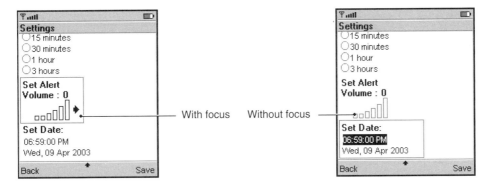

Figure 8.15 Interactive Gauge with and without User Focus

8.8.2 Progress Gauges

A progress gauge is a noninteractive gauge with a definite range. The application must supply a maximum value. The device maps the value of the gauge onto the display so that the user can see how close the current value is to the maximum value. Figure 8.16 shows a progress bar.

Figure 8.16 Progress Bar

The recommendations for progress bars are similar to the recommendations for interactive gauges. The difference is that MIDP implementors do not give users a way to change the value of a progress bar. Instead, the MIDP implementation updates the display of the progress bar as the application changes the gauge value.

8.8.3   Incremental Gauges

An application should use an incremental gauge when it can detect that it is making progress but does not know when the task will end. For example, if your application is receiving an unknown amount of pushed data, you can provide feedback that data is coming in, but not on how much longer it will be until the data transfer is done. In this case, an incremental gauge is appropriate. Incremental gauges do not have a defined range, so the application supplies the constant INDEFINITE as its maximum value.

Application Developers

 Strongly Recommend: Use an incremental gauge only if you can detect progress, but cannot determine how close the application is to its goal. If you can determine how close the application is to its goal (for example, if you can determine the percentage of work done), use a progress gauge, as described in "Progress Gauges" on page 111. If you cannot detect progress (for example, if you are waiting for a reply from a remote location), use a continuous gauge, as described in "Continuous Gauges" on page 113.

INCREMENTAL_UPDATING and INCREMENTAL_IDLE are the two states of an incremental gauge. The MIDP Reference Implementation uses the images shown in Figure 8.17 for these states.

Continuing with the example of receiving pushed data while the application receives data, you should use the incremental gauge's INCREMENTAL_UPDATING state. You would then update the gauge after each time your application receives a certain amount of data. You should change to the incremental-idle state when you have finished receiving the message and are closing connections, or preparing the message for display to the user.

 Strongly Recommend: Use the gauge's INCREMENTAL_UPDATING state while the task is taking place; use the INCREMENTAL_IDLE state when the long-running part of the task has completed and your application is cleaning up and preparing to move on to the next task.

Like a progress bar, the state of an incremental gauge changes in response to the application. Unlike a progress bar, however, the incremental gauge will not supply a value in a definite range. Instead, the application merely indicates that progress has been made.

MIDP Implementors

 Strongly Recommend: Make the appearance of an incremental gauge different from that of the progress gauge to reflect its different purpose. Use an animation for the INCREMENTAL_UPDATING state that implies progress toward a goal. For the INCREMENTAL_IDLE state, create a matching graphic that shows that no activity is occurring. Application developers often will use one followed by the other. For example, Figure 8.17 shows a tumbling figure; the goal is to cross the screen.

Figure 8.17 Incremental-Running and Incremental-Idle Gauges

 Strongly Recommend: Do not go to the next frame in an incremental-updating gauge until the application requests it.

8.8.4   Continuous Gauges

An application should use a continuous gauge when it cannot detect that it is making progress but needs to let the user know that the application is running and the device is not broken. For example, the MIDP Reference Implementation uses a continuous gauge when the user installs a MIDlet suite. When the installer contacts the server to download the JAR or JAD file, there is no way to know whether the server is making progress toward sending the requested file or how long the interaction will take. Continuous gauges do not have a defined range, so the application supplies the constant INDEFINITE as its maximum value.

Application Developers

Strongly Recommend: Use a continuous gauge only if you cannot detect progress. If you can detect progress, use either a progress gauge, as described in "Progress Gauges" on page 111, or an incremental gauge, as described in "Incremental Gauges" on page 112.

Consider: The danger in using a continuous-running gauge is that the application will never return and turn it off. This could happen if the operation never completes or your MIDlet crashes.

CONTINUOUS_RUNNING and CONTINUOUS_IDLE are the two states of a continuous gauge. The MIDP Reference Implementation uses the images shown in Figure 8.18 for these states.

Continuing with the example of getting a MIDlet suite's JAR or JAD file, while the installer contacts the server and waits for a reply, it uses the continuous gauge's CONTINUOUS_RUNNING state. After the file is downloaded, the installer uses the continuous gauge's CONTINUOUS_IDLE state while finishing the installation.

Strongly Recommend: Use the gauge's CONTINUOUS_RUNNING state while the task is taking place; use the CONTINUOUS_IDLE state when the long-running part of the task has completed and your application is cleaning up and preparing to move on to the next task.

MIDP Implementors

Strongly Recommend: Make the appearance of a continuous gauge different from the other gauges, to reflect its different purpose. Use a graphic for the CONTINUOUS_RUNNING state that implies activity without implying a state. Use a graphic for the CONTINUOUS_IDLE state that shows that no activity is occurring. Match the graphics because application developers will often use one followed by the other.

For example, in Figure 8.18, notice that Duke is waving his head for the CONTINUOUS_RUNNING state. The animation shows that activity is occurring, but it doesn't imply any particular progress toward the goal. The figure also shows Duke in the CONTINUOUS_IDLE state.

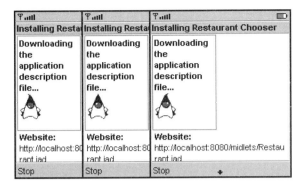

Figure 8.18 Continuous-Running and Continuous-Idle Gauges

 Strongly Recommend: Run and rerun the animation while the continuous gauge is in the CONTINUOUS_RUNNING state. Do not wait for a request from the application to go to the next frame.

8.8.5   Improving User Feedback From Noninteractive Gauges

Any time an application uses a noninteractive gauge, it should provide additional information to help the user understand the activity the gauge is tracking. If the activity is interruptible, the user should have the opportunity to stop it.

Application Developers

 Recommend: Use other items on the form to describe the purpose of the gauge, such as strings, additional graphics, and the gauge's label. Update the items as needed to give the user concise and immediate feedback. Figure 8.19 shows a form with a label, which describes the purpose of the gauge, and text strings to give the user additional feedback.

Figure 8.19 Additional Information on the Form with a Gauge

Application Developers, Continued

Strongly Recommend: When you use a gauge, provide a command of type STOP whenever possible. If the user chooses the command, cancel the operation in progress and give the user immediate feedback. This advice applies the design consideration, "Make Everything Interruptible" on page 13. (See Chapter 12 for more information on commands of type STOP.)

8.9   Choice Groups

A choice group is a set of selectable elements within a form. There are three types of choice groups:

- *Exclusive choice*: Allows a single choice from among elements that are always accessible. This is much like the exclusive-choice list, except that the list is a full-screen component. See "Exclusive-Choice Lists" on page 45 for advice on enabling a user to make a single selection from a group of elements.

- *Pop-up choice*: Allows a single choice from among items that, except for the selected element, are hidden until the user performs a device-specific action to show them. This kind of choice group does not have a full-screen counterpart.

- *Multiple choice*: Allows a user to choose zero or more elements. This kind of choice group is much like a multiple-choice list, except that the list is a full-screen component. See "Multiple-Choice Lists" on page 47 for advice on enabling a user to make multiple selections from a group of elements.

Application Developer Responsibilities	**MIDP Implementor Responsibilities**
• Any label text • Number of elements in the choice group • Any font suggestion • Any text associated with the elements • Any image associated with the elements • Which element or elements are preselected (The number of elements that can be selected is list-dependent.) • Any item-specific commands • Any default commands	• Handling scrolling or traversing (or both) through a choice group, if necessary • Determining how users select an element • Selection feedback • Text-display policy (single or multiline; wrapped, clipped, or scroll-through) • Height of the elements in the choice group • Informing the application when the user selects an element from a choice group

Application Developers

Consider: You can insert, delete, update, and set the selection of a choice group as needed. You can also add, update, or delete the choice group's label as needed. Try to make these changes only when the form is not visible or in response to a user action. Arbitrary changes to visible screens are confusing to users.

Strongly Recommend: Provide labels for choice groups. Have the labels tell users what they need to do with the choice group.

Recommend: Use a pop-up choice group when the user does not need to see all of the options all the time. You can also use a pop-up choice group for long lists of options because hiding all but the selected element saves screen real estate.

Recommend: When you try to decide whether to use a pop-up choice group or an exclusive-choice choice group, keep traversal in mind. Navigation through a pop-up choice group is a five-step process. The user must traverse to the choice group, perform the device-specific selection gesture, traverse to the correct option, perform the device-specific selection gesture again, and traverse out of the item. In contrast, it is only three steps to navigate through an exclusive-choice choice group. The user must traverse to the correct option in the choice group, perform the device-specific selection gesture, then traverse out of the item.

MIDP Implementors

Strongly Recommend: Provide different visual presentations for exclusive-choice, pop-up, and multiple-choice choice groups. For example, you might use radio buttons for the exclusive-choice mode, a pop-up menu for the pop-up choice mode, and check boxes for the multiple-choice mode. Figure 8.20 shows an example of different presentations.

 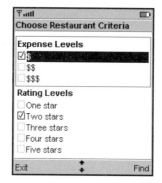 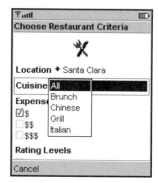

Figure 8.20 Presentations for Different Kinds of Choice Groups

Consider: You are permitted to use different visual representations for choice-groups and their full-screen counterparts, or the same visual representations. Having different looks is sometimes necessary to fit in with the native look-and-feel of the device. Having the same look makes the application more predictable. Figure 8.21 shows a choice group and its full-screen counterpart that have the same visual representation.

 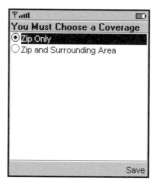

Figure 8.21 Exclusive-Choice on a Form and in a Screen

Other recommendations for using choice groups are the same as the recommendations for using lists, their screen counterparts. (See Chapter 5 for more information.)

8.10 Custom Items

A custom item is an item created by the application developer to be added to a form screen. For example, an application developer could use a custom item to create a media player, a map viewer, a combo box, and so on. Like a canvas (covered in Chapter 10) a custom item must be implemented carefully so that it is portable. It can be a valuable component if implemented carefully. Figure 8.22 shows a custom item, which shows a theater seating chart so that the user can choose a seat.

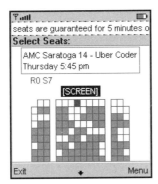

Figure 8.22 A Custom Item on a Form

Application Developer Responsibilities	MIDP Implementor Responsibilities
• Any label text • Visual appearance (fonts and colors) • Behavior • Sizing • Any traversal within the item content • Rendering • Responding to interactions from the user • Selection and traversal feedback	• Notifying the application when the user enters the custom item • Notifying the application when the user performs a scrolling or navigation gesture

Application Developers

Strongly Recommend: Provide a consistent visual appearance by using the same colors and fonts as the system. The system makes these attributes available, as well as the stroke style that it uses for drawing borders. (See *Programming Wireless Devices with the Java™ 2 Platform, Micro Edition* [17] for more information.)

Strongly Recommend: Supply minimum and preferred sizes to the form. Ensure that your item is usable at the minimum size. In addition to the minimum and preferred size you must provide a content size, so that the MIDP implementation can determine the bounding box of the custom item on the form.

MIDP Implementors

Strongly Recommend: Place labels outside the bounding box of the custom item. This enables you to maintain a consistent user interface for labels on form.

8.10.1   Traversal Into, Through, and Out of Custom Items

Since there is no way for a MIDP implementation to tell whether a custom item is interactive, it must support traversal into and out of custom items.

MIDP Implementors

Recommend: When a user traverses to a custom item, you should highlight it in case it is interactive. The visual representation of the highlight needs to be around but not on the custom item. It is possible that drawing a highlight on top of the custom item might interfere with its use. Figure 8.23 shows a custom item with a traversal highlight.

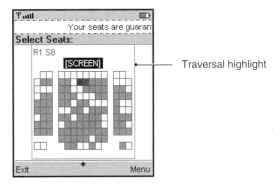

Figure 8.23 Custom Item with a Traversal Highlight

You can enable custom items to perform internal traversal, but you are not required to give custom items this option.

Strongly Recommend: Determine and publish whether your MIDP implementation will support internal traversal for custom items.

Strongly Recommend: If you support internal traversal for custom items, always check whether traversal is occurring. The developer supplies information on whether the traversal state within the custom item has changed with the user's last traversal action. If the custom item indicates that it is not responding to the traversal action, you should traverse to the next item on the form, if possible. (If the custom item is the first or last item on the form, it may not be possible for you to traverse to the next item. The user may have traversed as far as possible in the requested direction.)

Application Developers

You can, but are not required to, have your custom items support traversal. If there is no traversal possible within the custom item, the application developer can let the MIDP implementation know this (through a method's return value; see *Programming Wireless Devices with the Java™ 2 Platform, Micro Edition* [17] for more information). The implementation will then continue the traversal to the next item on the form.

Application Developers, Continued

 Strongly Recommend: If you support traversal within your custom items' content, provide users with obvious feedback so that they know where they are in the custom item. (See "Traversing and Scrolling Forms" on page 82 for advice on how to handle traversal through content.)

 Strongly Recommend: If you support traversal within your custom item, you must ensure that the user can traverse into and out of it. Test your MIDlet thoroughly to ensure that you have not created a trap that enables users to traverse into, but not out of, your custom item.

 Strongly Recommend: If your custom item contains content that the user can interact with, then provide clear highlight feedback to the user and support traversal within the content. (See "Traversal and Selection Highlighting" on page 85 and "Traversal Into, Through, and Out of Custom Items" on page 120 for more information.)

8.10.2 Interaction Modes for Custom Items

The *MIDP 2.0 Specification* [19] defines *interaction modes* for a custom item. They are a way for the MIDP implementation to inform the custom item of its capabilities. There are interaction mode constants for traversal, keypad input, and pointer input.

If a MIDP implementation supports traversal within a custom item, it informs the application by using either the TRAVERSE_HORIZONTAL or TRAVERSE_VERTICAL constant, or both.

If a MIDP implementation supports keypad input for custom items, it indicates this by using one or more of the constants KEY_PRESS, KEY_RELEASE, and KEY_REPEATED.

MIDP Implementors

 Strongly Recommend: Determine and publish whether you will support keypad input to a custom item. You are not required to support it at all, but if you support key release events, you must also support key press events. Similarly, if you support key repeated events, you must also support key press and key release events.

Strongly Recommend: If you support keypad input, you must be able to deliver events for the phone keypad keys. (That is, you must map the phone keypad events onto user actions, and deliver the events to the application.)

 Strongly Recommend: If you support keypad input, you must be able to map keypad input onto game actions. You are also permitted to provide access to device-specific key events.

The set of keys and the key events available to a custom item may differ from what is available on a canvas, as may the mapping between key codes and game actions. For example, if your device supports traversal, you might use the left, right, up, and down keys for traversal instead of delivering these key events to custom items. You might also change which key events are available to an application depending on whether the custom item has a command associated with it.

If a MIDP implementation supports touch input, it indicates this by using one or more of the constants `POINTER_PRESS`, `POINTER_RELEASE`, and `POINTER_DRAG`.

 Strongly Recommend: Determine and publish whether you will support touch input to a custom item. You are not required to support touch input to a custom item. If you do support pointer release events, however, you must also support pointer press events. Similarly, if you support pointer drag events, you must also support pointer press and pointer release events.

The MIDP Reference Implementation supports all interaction modes except horizontal traversal and touch input. It maps the Select key to the default command if there is one associated with the custom item.

 Strongly Recommend: Using different buttons to activate the default commands of different items is likely to result in very poor usability. Ideally, activating a custom item should be consistent with the way other form items are activated.

 Strongly Recommend: Consider the behaviors you provide to other items on a form when you choose which interaction modes to make available to a custom item. Indiscriminately mixing interaction modes can result in serious usability problems.

Application Developers

Strongly Recommend: Design your custom item so that it indicates to users how to use the interaction modes. For example, provide Help screens. Users will need clear hints to understand how to operate a custom item.

Recommend: Have users edit your custom item in place on the form (using one or more interaction modes) or off the form. You should support both modes to ensure that the item can be edited across a variety of platforms.

For example, you might implement a custom item that a user can edit in place using touch input. At runtime, you should query the system to determine whether it supports your interaction mode. If it does, you can have the user edit the custom item in place; otherwise, you can have the user edit the item off the form.

> *Consider*: If you want the user to be able to edit your custom item with full interaction, you could make the custom item display-only and use a canvas as an offscreen editor. (Canvases are covered in Chapter 10.) This could result in a more consistent user interface across devices, though potentially more complex to interact with.

If you do this, use an item-specific abstract command to invoke a separate editing screen. Make it the custom element's default command so that it is easy and fast to use. When the user issues a command on the Editing screen that indicates that editing is complete (or canceled), you can incorporate any edits into the custom item, and return to the form.

MIDP Implementors

Strongly Recommend: If there is a default command assigned to a custom item, determine which key the user must press to initiate the command. The set of keys and the key events available to a custom item may differ from what is available on a canvas.

CHAPTER **9**

Alerts

AN alert is a screen that communicates error, status, or other information to users. An alert screen, like other screens, can have titles, tickers, and commands. It can also have an image, a gauge, and text the user cannot edit. Most commonly, alerts are expected to have titles, images, and text. Figure 9.1 shows an informational alert with these characteristics.

Figure 9.1 Alert Screen with Title, Image, and Text

Application Developer Responsibilities	MIDP Implementor Responsibilities
• Any label text • Alert text, graphic, gauge • Any commands • Any command listener • Alert type • Whether the alert should be modal or (if possible) timed • Requested duration for a timed alert	• Fonts and colors used on the screen • Placement of any graphic or gauge • Default time to display a timed alert • Any sound associated with an alert • Default command label for modal alert • Default command listener • Differentiate between alert types

Application Developers

Consider: You can change the alert type, title, text, image, and gauge, as needed. In addition, you can change between requesting a *timed* or *modal* alert, as needed (a timed alert stays visible for only a designated period of time; a modal alert requires the user to dismiss it).

 Strongly Recommend: Use modal alerts only when the user must see and acknowledge the alert. This is the case for alerts that: report serious errors, that warn when data loss might occur, or that ask for confirmation before performing an operation. This advice applies the design consideration, "Minimize Interruptions From MIDP and MIDlets" on page 13.

 Strongly Recommend: Do not use tickers in alerts. Tickers distract from the alert message. If you interrupt the user with an alert, the message is important; the user should not be distracted. In addition, alerts are frequently pop-up windows, whereas tickers appear anchored to a screen. The two are incompatible.

MIDP Implementors

Design the layout of both timed and modal alerts. Some devices have timed and modal alerts that look different from each other. For example, some use a timer graphic to indicate that an alert is timed. Other devices make timed alerts look like modal alerts, except for the absence of a button to dismiss the alert, as shown in Figure 9.2.

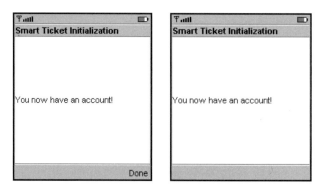

Figure 9.2 Modal and Timed Alerts with a Similar Look

Recommend: Make your timed alert different from your modal alert, if this would be consistent with the user interface of your device. For example, the timed alert could be a pop-up window, while the modal alert could look more like the other high-level screens. The difference will give users an obvious cue as to whether they just need to wait until the alert disappears or they need to respond.

Consider: If an application provides a ticker, but device restrictions or conventions preclude putting a ticker on an alert, you are not required to display it.

9.1   Titles for Alert Screens

Application Developers

 Recommend: Use a title for modal alerts. For example, an error alert could have as its title the type of error, while the text of the alert could explain the problem. Figure 9.3 shows an example of the alert. It is less critical for a timed alert to use a title.

Figure 9.3 Modal Alert with a Title

MIDP Implementors

Consider: Ensure that your alert screens are understandable without reading the alert title. Usability studies show that users may ignore or overlook screen titles.

9.2   Text of Alerts

The text in an alert should be succinct. This will help get the information across to consumers, even though they might not have much time and might not be able to give the device their full attention.

If an alert has a long text, consumers must be given as much time as they need to read the message.

MIDP Implementors

Strongly Recommend: Display alerts that require scrolling as modal alerts. Application developers can request either timed or modal alerts, but if they give an alert so much content such that it must scroll, make the alert modal.

Application Developers

Recommend: Avoid having a timed alert become a modal alert by keeping messages for timed alerts short, such as from one to three words. Given the many screen sizes of devices and the different fonts they may use, there is no guarantee that a timed alert will never be turned into a modal alert. Keeping messages short and testing the application on a device with a small screen (such as one with 96-by-54 pixels) gives an application developer the best chance of keeping timed alerts timed.

9.3   Duration of Alerts

A modal alert has a duration of FOREVER. A timed alert, by default, uses the default duration of the device.

MIDP Implementors

Strongly Recommend: Choose default durations for timed alerts that are long enough to allow the user to read a screen full of text, but short enough not to frustrate the user's progress through the application. Because timed alerts have little text it is reasonable to expect users to need one-half to two seconds to read them. The actual default is best determined through usability testing on the device.

Application Developers

 Recommend: Use the MIDP implementor's default duration for timed alerts. An application is more portable if a timed alert's duration is device-specific, not application-specific.

9.4   Gauges in Alerts

An application developer can associate a gauge with an alert to show activity or progress. For example, Figure 9.4 shows an alert that uses a gauge to let the user know that activity is taking place.

Figure 9.4   Alert with a Progress Gauge

 Strongly Recommend: Gauges in an alert must be noninteractive. Appropriate gauges to show that activity is taking place are continuous, incremental, and progress.

 Strongly Recommend: Gauges used in an alert cannot have a label, layout directives, or a set height or width. You cannot associate a command with the gauge (although you can associate commands with the alert). In other words, you cannot set item attributes for a gauge in an alert, as you can for one in a form.

See "Gauges" on page 107 for more information on gauges and how to use them.

9.5   Abstract Commands on Alert Screens

Application developers can associate one or more abstract commands with an alert screen. One reason to associate an abstract command with an alert is to provide a label for dismissing the alert. Another time is to enable the user to stop a currently running process.

9.5.1   Labeling the Dismissal of an Alert

A MIDP implementation has no way to know the text of your alert, and therefore cannot provide an application-specific label. Application developers that want a particular label on an alert can provide an abstract command with that label.

Application Developers

> *Consider*: Provide an abstract command to dismiss your alerts so that the dismissal label can be specific to your application. For example, Figure 9.5 shows an application-defined label. Provide the command even when you request a timed alert. You will then have an application-defined label in case a MIDP implementation must present the alert as modal for some reason.

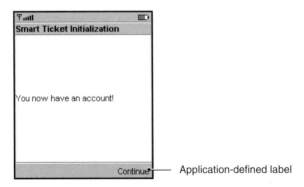

Figure 9.5 Application-Defined Soft Label to Dismiss a Modal Alert

Recommend: Use the abstract command types OK and CANCEL where they are appropriate. (See page 137 for more information.)

 Recommend: Do not give an alert more than two commands. More commands will result in the user having to access a system menu or other user-interface component to dismiss the alert. This makes your application less usable.

 Strongly Recommend: If you provide an abstract command for an alert, it must dismiss the alert. If you provide more than one abstract command, at least one of the commands must dismiss the alert. (See "Abstract Commands on Alert Screens" on page 130 for more information.)

If the application developer does not provide an abstract command to dismiss the alert, the MIDP implementation must determine how to dismiss it. Typically, the MIDP implementation provides a label for a soft button or key on the device.

MIDP Implementors

 Recommend: Choose neutral labels for any buttons or keys that dismiss modal dialog boxes. A neutral label is best because you have no way of knowing what message alerts will display. Figure 9.6 shows an example of a neutral label on a modal alert.

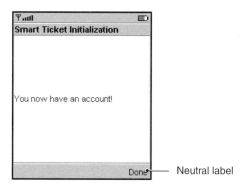

Figure 9.6 Label for a Soft Button to Dismiss a Modal Alert

The presence of a single abstract command should not be sufficient to change a timed alert into a modal alert.

Strongly Recommend: If the application developer has provided one abstract command and requested a timed alert, make the alert timed if possible. If the alert must be modal for device-specific reasons (such as the text causing the alert to scroll), then use the application's abstract command for the user to dismiss the alert.

The presence of multiple abstract commands, however, means that the alert should be modal.

Consider: If the application developer has both provided multiple abstract commands and requested a timed alert, make the alert modal and use the application's abstract commands for the user to dismiss the alert.

9.5.2   Enabling Users to Stop an Action

Another reason to provide an abstract command on an alert is to enable the user to stop a potentially long-running action. An application developer that wanted this behavior would typically put the abstract command on an alert with a gauge, so that the user could get feedback as the long-running action is carried out.

Application Developers

Consider: Use a modal alert to enable a user to interrupt an operation in progress. Provide an abstract command of type STOP for the interruption. The alert in Figure 9.7 has a command of type STOP (it has the label "Stop") to enable the user to interrupt the operation in progress.

Figure 9.7   Alert with a Command of Type STOP

Consider: When you give an alert a command of type STOP, and the operation reaches a point where the user can no longer interrupt it, remove the abstract command. You can also request that the alert be timed at this point.

9.6 Command Listeners for Alerts

All alerts must have a command listener. The *command listener* is the object that receives the notification that the alert has timed out (if the alert is timed) or that the user has chosen an abstract command associated with the alert (if the alert is modal). At least one of the commands that the command listener handles must *dismiss the alert*. To dismiss the alert means to change the current screen from the alert to the next application-specified screen.

Application Developers

Strongly Recommend: If you must do an application-specific task as the result of dismissing an alert, or if you provide multiple abstract commands, provide a command listener. The command listener must do the application-specific task then set the next screen (the screen that takes the place of the alert).

Consider: You can provide a command listener whether or not you attach an application-specific abstract command to the alert. For example, you would do this if you have to do an application-specific action but are content to use the MIDP implementor's label.

MIDP Implementors

Strongly Recommend: Provide a default command listener for alerts that have a single abstract command but no application-specific command listener. The command listener must advance the MIDlet to the next screen when the user dismisses the alert or the alert times out.

9.7   Alert Types

All alerts can have an associated *alert type*, which the application developer can provide, to give the MIDP implementation an indication of the function of the alert. An alert type is a typesafe enumeration that has the following constants: INFO, WARNING, ERROR, ALARM, and CONFIRMATION, as described in the upcoming sections.

Application Developers

 Recommend: Give your alerts an alert type whenever possible. Associating an alert type with an alert enables your MIDlet to take advantage of any visual and auditory specialization of a MIDP implementation.

MIDP Implementors

 Recommend: Differentiate alert types clearly to users. Do this through the use of layout, sounds, and so on. Giving the user visual and auditory cues as to the nature of an alert can make applications easier to use.

Another way to differentiate alert types is with images. (Many alerts in the upcoming figures have an image that reinforces its purpose.)

Consider: If you use images to differentiate alert types, determine and publish how they will work with any images the application provides. For example, MIDP for Palm OS had images that it used to differentiate the alert types, unless the application provided an image. If the application provided an image, it used that image instead.

9.7.1   INFO Alert Type

The INFO alert type is designed for providing nonthreatening information. In the MIDP Reference Implementation, there is no sound associated with an INFO alert. Figure 9.8 shows an INFO alert.

Figure 9.8 An Alert with an INFO Alert Type

Application Developers

> *Consider*: Use INFO alert types to display About boxes and Splash screens.

9.7.2 WARNING Alert Types

The WARNING alert type is designed for informing the user about potentially danger-
ous operations. In the MIDP Reference Implementation, a WARNING alert plays a
tone. Figure 9.9 shows a WARNING alert.

Figure 9.9 An Alert with a WARNING Alert Type

Application Developers

> *Consider*: Use a WARNING alert type to let the user know about actions that might require an application to restart or that could result in data loss.

> *Consider*: Make alerts of type WARNING modal.

9.7.3   ERROR Alert Type

The ERROR alert type is designed for showing users error messages. In the MIDP Reference Implementation, an ERROR alert plays a tone. Figure 9.10 shows an ERROR alert.

Figure 9.10 An Alert with an ERROR Alert Type

Application Developers

> *Consider*: Application developers should consider using ERROR alert types to tell users about errors that the system cannot correct.

> *Strongly Recommend*: Make alerts of type ERROR modal. If the error is severe enough to warrant interrupting the user, the user should be able to take as much time as necessary to read and understand the information. A user can keep the modal dialog open indefinitely.

9.7.4   ALARM Alert Type

The ALARM alert type is designed to alert users to events about which they had asked to be notified. In the MIDP Reference Implementation, an ALARM alert plays a tone. Figure 9.11 shows an alert with an ALARM alert type.

Figure 9.11 An Alert with an ALARM Alert Type

Application Developers

> *Consider*: Use ALARM alert types to inform users only when they have previously requested the alert. Use this alert type in conjunction with MIDP's timer and alarm functionality.

> *Recommend*: Make alerts of type ALARM modal so that you can be sure users got the information they requested.

9.7.5   CONFIRMATION Alert Type

The CONFIRMATION alert type is designed to provide information so that a user can confirm that a particular event should occur. Figure 9.12 shows an alert with a CONFIRMATION alert type.

Figure 9.12 An Alert with a CONFIRMATION Alert Type

Application Developers

Consider: Use a CONFIRMATION alert type on a modal alert to ask users to confirm operations that may cost money, use airtime, or change data. Give the alert two abstract commands (one of type OK and the other of type CANCEL; see "Abstract Commands" starting on page 165 for more information) and provide labels appropriate for the task. For example, Figure 9.12 shows an alert that allows the user to decide whether to continue with an operation that would cost money.

CHAPTER 10

Canvas Screens

A canvas provides access to low-level input mechanisms, such as key presses and low-level graphics calls, such as drawing simple shapes. A canvas can be useful to an application that needs full control of the screen. It can be used as a way to edit or display a custom item off the form, for example. SmartTicket uses a canvas, shown in Figure 10.1, for the screen that enables a user to choose a seat in the theater. The canvas displays a graphic of a floor plan.

Figure 10.1 SmartTicket's Canvas Screen

MIDP 2.0 also provides an extension to Canvas screens, called a game canvas. The game canvas has additional features such as sprites, background panning, layers, and an offscreen buffer. The advice in this chapter also applies to the games canvas (except for the discussion on creating your own offscreen buffer); additional advice, specific to the game canvas, is covered in Chapter 11.

Application Developer Responsibilities	MIDP Implementor Responsibilities
• Drawing the screen • Updating the screen as necessary (for example, in response to key presses) • Abstract commands for the screen	• Mapping game actions to the device • Support for phone keypad keys • Touch input support (if available on the device) • Informing the application of user input (key input, touch input, abstract command use)

Because a canvas provides access to lower-level functionality, an application developer can create a screen that is tuned for a particular device. It is also possible, by following the guidelines in this chapter, to create portable applications that use a canvas screen. The advice will also help in creating canvas screens that integrate well with high-level screens in an application.

10.1   Title and Ticker

A canvas screen can have a title and ticker, just as the high-level screens do. The title and ticker take away space from the content region of a canvas screen, however. The canvas has more space for content without them. Notice the difference in the space available for the drawing of the game screen in Figure 10.2. Displaying a canvas without a title or ticker is called *full-screen mode*. (See "Full-Screen Mode" on page 38 for more information on how the screen can change.)

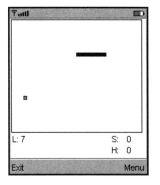 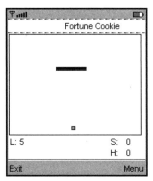

Figure 10.2   WormGame Canvas with and without a Title or Ticker

Application Developers

Strongly Recommend: Decide whether to use a title or ticker before displaying the canvas. If you go to full-screen mode after a canvas has been displayed, the canvas will have to be redrawn. Redrawing the canvas to resize the content area interrupts the user and can be disconcerting.

10.2 Key Events

A device must support key events for both *game actions* and the keys of an ITU-T standard telephone keypad. Game actions are device-independent key events representing up, down, left, right, select/fire, A, B, C, and D. The ITU-T standard telephone keypad corresponds to key events for the digits 0 to 9, and the symbols pound (#) and star (∗).

MIDP Implementors

Strongly Recommend: Decide and publish how you will map key events onto the device.

Consider: Consider game actions the default input mechanism for canvases and make them consistent with the device. For example, Sun's MIDP for Palm OS maps the left, right, up, down, and select/fire keys to those commonly used by native game applications for these functions, as shown in Figure 10.3.

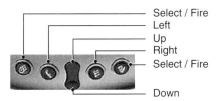

Figure 10.3 Mapping of Common Game Actions on a PDA

Key-event mappings for the phone keypad might be more natural on one device than on another. For example, they map directly onto a phone, but not onto a device with a QWERTY keyboard or a device with no alphanumeric keypad. A device with a QWERTY keyboard could map the digit keys to the row of numbers above the keyboard, as shown in Figure 10.4.

Number keys for the digit key events

Figure 10.4   Mapping the Digit Key Events onto a QWERTY Keyboard

A device with no alphanumeric keypad, such as a PDA with touch input, could support the phone keypad by creating a touch-sensitive onscreen representation that the user can display on the screen, as shown in Figure 10.5.

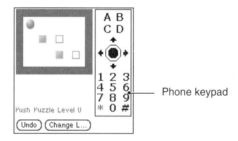

Phone keypad

Figure 10.5   Onscreen Representation of a Phone Keypad on a PDA

Application Developers

Strongly Recommend: Use game actions instead of the phone keypad whenever possible because game actions are more usable across devices. For example, consumers that must show and use the keypad shown in Figure 10.5 report in usability testing that it feels awkward to use. It is not a Palm OS standard and shares the screen with the application, decreasing the application's display size.

The game actions up, down, left, right, and select/fire are familiar to many consumers because they are commonly used by games. There are no standard uses for the game actions A, B, C, and D, however. (They might be seen as roughly equivalent to the extra keys on game machines, sometimes labeled A, B, L, and R. These keys too are used as the game finds necessary.)

> *Consider*: Publish your use of game actions or the phone keypad keys for consumers. Provide Help screens for Canvas screens, especially when you use the game actions A, B, C, and D. Consumers have no way of knowing from prior experience what A, B, C, and D do. Explaining the functions of the game actions or phone keypad lets consumers enjoy the application rather than getting frustrated figuring out how to operate it.

10.3   Touch Input

Some devices, such as PDAs, have touch input. It is not available on all devices, however. If a device has touch input, it should be incorporated into the canvas screens of applications so that these screens can behave like native applications and like the high-level screens of MIDP. (See "Touch Input" on page 231 for more information.)

10.4   Colors, Fonts, Shapes, and Images

Application developers control what appears on a canvas screen: images, text, and simple shapes. They also control attributes such as the colors used, the fonts, whether lines are drawn with solid or dotted strokes, and so on.

10.4.1 Images

The guidelines for images drawn onto a canvas are the same as those for image items on forms: Images should be in PNG (portable network graphics) format, and application developers should consider saving them with limited colors to conserve resources. (See "Images" on page 92 for detailed information.)

10.4.2 Screen Attributes

For high-level screens, the MIDP implementation sets the colors, the stroke style used for drawing borders, and the font. (Application developers can request a font for some high-level entities, such as elements in lists, but there is no guarantee that the request will be honored.) The MIDP implementation makes its use of colors, fonts, and border styles available to the application developer.

Application Developers

> *Consider*: If your application uses both canvas and high-level screens, provide a consistent visual appearance by using the same colors, fonts, and border styles as the system.

10.4.3 Coordinate System

Drawing on a canvas involves providing values such as the coordinates at which the object should be drawn, sometimes a height or a width, and so on. This requires an understanding of the coordinate system. The coordinate system has its origin at the upper-left corner. The X coordinates increase left to right, and the Y coordinates increase top to bottom, as shown in Figure 10.6.

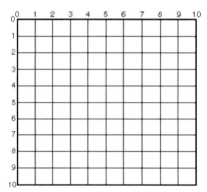

Figure 10.6 Coordinate System

The coordinates specify the points between pixels. The pixel at (1,1), then, would be drawn below and to the right of coordinate (1,1). It is the pixel bounded by the coordinates (1,1), (1,2), (2,1), and (2,2). Figure 10.7 shows that pixel.

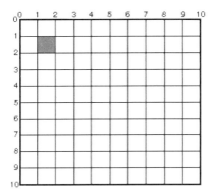

Figure 10.7 A Pixel in the Coordinate System

10.4.4 Drawing and Filling Operations

Drawing a line in the coordinate system touches pixels at both ends. For example, drawing a line from the points (0,3) to (0,5) is three pixels long. Drawing a line from the points (1,1) to (1,1) would result in drawing the pixel shown in Figure 10.7.

Because of the coordinate system and the way that the drawing of lines is specified, filled and drawn (unfilled) shapes have different sizes. An unfilled shape is one pixel larger in width and height than a filled one.

MIDP Implementors

Strongly Recommend: To fill a rectangle with the origin (0,0), height 6, and width 8, fill in the pixels between coordinates (0,0), (0,8), (6,0), and (6,8), as shown in Figure 10.8. That is, starting at point (0,0) fill in the rectangle is made by drawing eight pixels right and six pixels down.

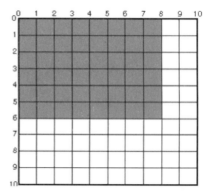

Figure 10.8 Filled Rectangle

Strongly Recommend: To draw a rectangle with the same origin, height, and width, draw it as though you are drawing lines from the pixel at point (0,0) to the pixel at point (0,8), from the pixel at point (8,0) to the pixel at point (8,6), and so on. The effect is that the height will be one pixel taller than the difference between Y coordinates, and the width will be one pixel longer than the difference between X coordinates. Figure 10.9 shows a rectangle that has been drawn.

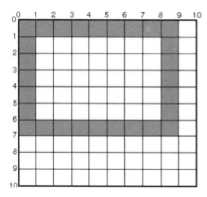

Figure 10.9 Drawing a Rectangle

Application Developers and MIDP Implementors

Strongly Recommend: To draw a filled rectangle and a drawn rectangle that are the same size, you must request rectangles with different heights and widths. For example, consider an object like a progress gauge, which has a row of rectangles all of the same size, some of which are filled and some of which are drawn, as shown in Figure 10.10. If the filled rectangles to the left were drawn with a height of 15 and a width of 4, the hollow rectangles to the right would be drawn with a height of 14 and a width of 3.

Figure 10.10   Progress Gauge with Same-Size Hollow and Filled Rectangles

10.4.5   Anchor Points

Drawing a string or an image requires not only a coordinate but also an *anchor point*. An anchor point is a combination of a horizontal value (LEFT, RIGHT, or HCENTER) and a vertical value (TOP, BOTTOM, or VCENTER) that indicates which part of the string or image should be placed at the coordinate. Figure 10.10 shows the various anchor points.

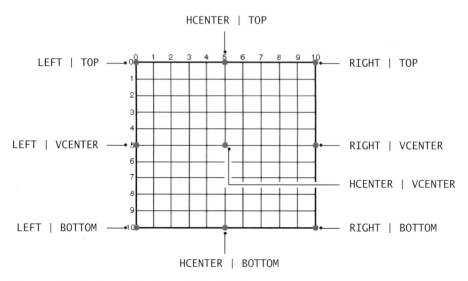

Figure 10.11   Anchor Points and Their Effects

Application Developers and MIDP Implementors

 Strongly Recommend: Do not use the VCENTER value when specifying an anchor point for a string. (You can use any value when specifying an anchor point for an image.)

10.5   Accommodating Different Screen Sizes

Relying on a particular screen size is inadvisable even for application developers who are designing an application for a specific MID. Even a single device can give an application different amounts of the screen at different times. For example, in Sun's MIDP for Palm OS, consumers can turn on application buttons or game controls, both of which impact the amount of available screen real estate. Figure 10.12 shows the Push Puzzle game with and without the phone keypad on the screen. Changes in screen size can also take place if an application moves to and from full-screen mode.

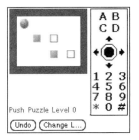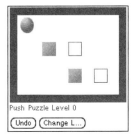

Figure 10.12   Unstructured Screen with and without Phone Keypad

Application Developers:

 Strongly Recommend: Do not assume a particular size of device screen when designing a Canvas screen. Applications that assume a particular size of screen are not necessarily portable.

Even if you assume a small screen size, your application will not necessarily be usable on all MIDs. For example, Figure 10.13 shows a Push Puzzle game that expects a small screen. It is awkward when displayed on a mobile phone with a larger screen.

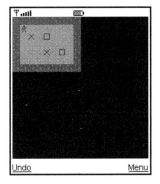

Figure 10.13   Canvas Designed for a Small Screen on a Large Screen

Consider: Use a scaled graphic instead of a bitmap, when possible, for graphics that will be drawn onto a canvas. Because different MIDs have different screen sizes, an application that uses a small scalable graphic and then scales it up for larger screens is more portable.

10.6   Avoiding Flicker

When the contents of a screen seem to blink or seem unsteady, the screen is said to flicker. Flicker is annoying to users and can actually be harmful to persons with photosensitive epilepsy if the flicker occurs at a rate of 2 to 55 flashes per second. This section offers some guidelines for avoiding flicker.

Application Developers

 Recommend: When you create an application that draws to the screen, minimize flicker by organizing your data to support redrawing as little of the screen as possible.

For example, SmartTicket draws a seating chart onto a canvas so that users can choose seats in a theater. Users can navigate through the empty seats, select seats, and change their selections. There are many ways to represent the data that makes this possible. (The data includes the number of rows in the theater, the number of seats per row, the status of each seat, and so on.) The following paragraphs describe two ways to organize this data; they require a very different amount of redrawing.

One way to represent the data on the Canvas screen is with an array. Each row of the array would correspond to a row in the theater. Cells could correspond to seats (such as current, occupied, unoccupied) and nonseat spaces (such as aisles). Each time the user moves from one empty seat to another, the application would have to find the cell for the user's current seat, update its status, find the cell representing the next unoccupied seat in the direction in which the user navigated, update its status, use the array data to recompute the color of each pixel on the canvas, and redraw the entire canvas. Having to do this much work could cause flicker.

Another way to represent the data for the canvas screen is to have, in addition to the array, fields for the old and new seat locations. Using this data organization, the application could do much less work. Each time the user moves from one empty seat to another, it would retrieve the user's current location (instead of searching for it), update the status of that cell, find the next unoccupied seat in the direction in which the user navigated, update that cell's status, recompute the colors of the pixels that correspond to the old and new seats (instead of the whole screen), and request repaints of the areas containing the updated pixels (instead of the whole screen). This data organization means less computation and repainting and helps to minimize flicker.

10.6.1 Double-Buffering

Double-buffering is another way to minimize flickering of the screen. A device that provides double-buffering draws your requested updates onto an image that is not the screen. This image is called a *buffer*, or *backing store*. The device updates the screen by transferring (painting) the buffer onto the screen. The device can transfer the image quickly, minimizing flickering and delays in screen updates.

Application Developers

Recommend: Create applications that use double-buffering. Simulate it with an application buffer or use a game canvas if it is not available on a Canvas screen. To simulate double-buffering, create a buffer (an image) within the application, draw to it, then paint the screen from the buffer.

Consider: Try to both use double-buffering and minimize the area that you need to redraw. If you use double-buffering but do not try to minimize the size of the update area, you could end up recalculating and redrawing the entire buffer before transferring it onto the screen. The delay caused by the calculations could cause flicker or make the device seem unresponsive. Similarly, if you minimize the update area but do not use double-buffering, you might still get some flicker.

MIDP Implementors

Recommend: Provide double-buffering whenever possible, and publish the feature for application developers. Include a list of exceptions, such as the amount of available memory.

10.6.2 Batch Paint Requests

In addition to the techniques used by application developers, MIDP implementors can also help to minimize flickering and resource usage.

MIDP Implementors

Recommend: Process paint requests in batches to minimize resource usage. Batching paint requests merges the parts of the screen that each paint request would have affected (called *clipping regions*) into a single clipping region. The batched request affects all parts of the screen that the individual paint requests would have affected.

For example, as the user navigates through the SmartTicket canvas, the application could make two repaint requests for each move: one would request that the old seat be repainted and the other would request that the new seat be repainted. If the MIDP implementation did not batch paint requests, redrawing the old and new seats would result in two separate screen paintings. Batching the requests would have the screen redraw the rectangle created by the old and new seat locations, possibly saving resources. Figure 10.14 shows an old seat location, a new seat location, and the rectangle that results from combining their clipping regions.

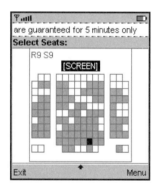 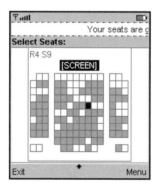 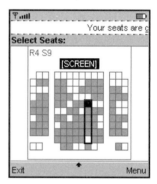

Figure 10.14   Rectangle Redrawn between Two Selectable Seats

Application Developers

Consider: When you write the code for your canvas's `paint` methods, check the clipping region in case the MIDP implementation has batched paint requests. You cannot assume a one-to-one correspondence between your calls to the `repaint` methods and the system's calls to the canvas's `paint` method. If the MIDP implementation batches repaint requests, the `paint` method could be asked to paint a seemingly arbitrary portion of the screen.

If you do not check the clipping region, you could try to repaint too much of the screen or miss repainting part of the screen. If you try to repaint too much of the screen (that is, if you don't check the clipping region, but instead have the `repaint` method try to redraw the entire screen each time), you would waste resources. If you miss repainting parts of the screen, the application will not respond properly to the user's key presses or screen taps, making the application unusable.

For example, assume that you wrote the `paint` method for the example shown in Figure 10.14 as though it would only ever be asked to repaint a single seat. (That is, assume that you wrote the `paint` method as though there would be a one-to-one correspondence between the application's requests to repaint the screen and calls to the `paint` method.) If the MIDP implementation batched the paint requests, as shown in Figure 10.14, your application might clear the old seat location but not draw the new location. The MIDlet would not respond properly to the user's key presses or touches.

CHAPTER 11

Game Screens, Layers, and Sprites

THE game package is new in MIDP 2.0. The package has a game canvas, which extends the capabilities of a canvas in ways that make it more convenient to write games and other applications. It is useful in situations where a consistent level of performance is important. For example, arcade games are good candidates for using the game canvas.

Other reasons that an application developer would use a game canvas instead of a regular canvas are offscreen buffering, *key latching*, and *key suppression*. (These are the same features that help the game canvas achieve its performance consistency.)

The recommendations given in Chapter 10 for canvases also apply to game screens. This chapter provides additional recommendations.

Application Developer Responsibilities	MIDP Implementor Responsibilities
• Drawing the screen • Updating the screen as necessary (for example, in response to key presses) • Abstract commands for the screen • Any text to be used in the ticker of the screen • Any text to be used in the title of the screen	• Game actions • Phone keypad keys • Touch input (if the device supports it) • Providing an offscreen buffer • Informing the application of user input (pressing a game action or phone keypad button, or tapping a touch screen)

11.1   Offscreen Buffer

Using an offscreen buffer can be part of an application developer's flicker-prevention strategy. Game canvases always provide an offscreen buffer. MIDP implementations provide it, even when the device does not support double buffering. A regular canvas, in contrast, need not have an offscreen buffer. (See Chapter 10 for more information.)

Use the offscreen buffer as the single source for what is rendered on the screen.

MIDP Implementors

Strongly Recommend: By default, paint the game screen with the contents of the offscreen buffer.

Application Developers

Strongly Recommend: Put your application's initial game-screen content (such as a Splash screen or the initial Game screen) into the offscreen buffer before making the game canvas visible. The offscreen buffer is initially filled with white pixels. If you wait until after the game canvas is made visible to put content into the offscreen buffer, the user will initially see a blank screen. Users could perceive this as a performance problem, or as a broken application.

11.2   Key Latching and Suppression

Using key latching enables an application developer to efficiently determine whether the user has pressed a key since the last time through the game loop. Key suppression keeps the regular event loop from handling actions for the game canvas. Suppressing events can improve performance by eliminating unnecessary system calls to the `keyPressed`, `keyRepeated`, and `keyReleased` methods.

Application Developers

Recommend: Use key latching and key suppression together to save both time and memory.

11.3   Layers

In addition to the game canvas, the game package provides *layers*, which are basic visual elements on a game screen. One type of layer is a *sprite*. Another type is a *tiled* layer, which enables an application developer to construct a single image from smaller individual images. The game package also provides a *layer manager* for applications that use multiple layers or that have layers larger than the device screen.

11.3.1   Sprites

A sprite is an image comprised of frames (smaller images). When an application draws a sprite, it draws one of the frames. An application can show different frames in a sequence to animate the sprite. The sprites in MIDP also provide transformations, such as mirroring, and collision detection.

Application Developer

Recommend: Use sprites for animation. Don't try to create your own animation code. The sprites in a MIDP implementation provide additional features, such as collision detection and transformations. They will also be tuned to perform well on their devices.

Sprites provide transformations such as rotating 90 degrees. They provide the concept of a *reference pixel* so that the transformations can appear to be taking place around a certain place in the sprite.

Strongly Recommend: Remember that the transformation of a sprite is around the reference *pixel*, not a reference point. A point is an (x,y) position on the canvas. A pixel is the pixel below and to the right of the point that defines it. (It is in the space defined by the points (x,y), (x+1,y), (x,y+1), (x+1,y+1).) (See Chapter 10 for more information.)

When an application developer positions a sprite at an initial x and y point, the point sets the location of the upper-left corner of the sprite's visual bounds. It puts the sprite's top, left pixel at the pixel below and to the right of the (x,y) position on the canvas, as shown in Figure 11.1.

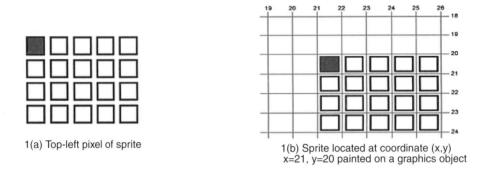

1(a) Top-left pixel of sprite

1(b) Sprite located at coordinate (x,y)
x=21, y=20 painted on a graphics object

Figure 11.1 Positioning a Sprite

By contrast, setting a reference around which to transform a sprite requires an application developer to provide an x and a y value, but the values define the position of a reference *pixel*, as shown in Figure 11.2, not a point.

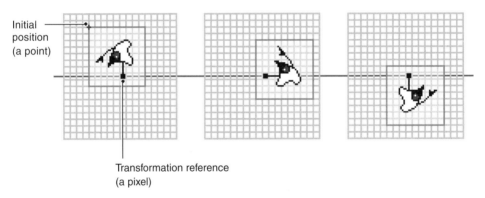

Initial position (a point)

Transformation reference (a pixel)

Figure 11.2 A Sprite's Reference Pixel

Another feature of sprites is collision detection, which takes place within a collision rectangle. By default the rectangle is the entire sprite, but the application developer can make the rectangle smaller or larger. Collision detection checks for an intersection between the collision rectangle and an image, a nonempty tile in a tiled layer, or another sprite. Collision detection can also be done at the pixel level. In this case, the algorithm checks for collisions using only opaque pixels in the collision rectangle and the other tile, sprite, or image.

Application Developers

Strongly Recommend: Minimize your use of pixel-level collision detection. It may be less efficient to check for collisions at this level than for an intersection of the entities' boundaries.

11.3.2 Tiled Layers

Tiled layers provide an alternative to using large images in games. A tiled layer is a graphic made up of individual rectangles, and a group of small images that are the same size as the rectangles. The individual tiles are written into the rectangle in the order specified by the application developer. Figure 11.3 shows how tiles can be written to a tiled layer to form a larger picture.

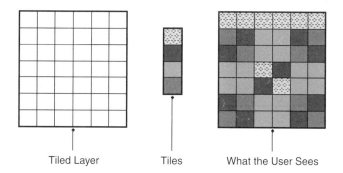

Tiled Layer   Tiles   What the User Sees

Figure 11.3 Tiled Layer and Tiles

Using a few individual tiles over and over to form a picture allows a game to use fewer system resources than would be used by a single large graphic. Using tiles can minimize screen redrawing and require less storage space on the device than a large picture would.

Application Developers

Recommend: In order to minimize resource requirements and improve performance, use tiles whenever possible to create your background images. For instance, the Push Puzzle example with the MIDP Reference

Implementation uses tiled layers. Each level is simply a different arrangement of the tiles (as shown in Figure 11.4), and each theme is a new set of tiles (as shown in Figure 11.5).

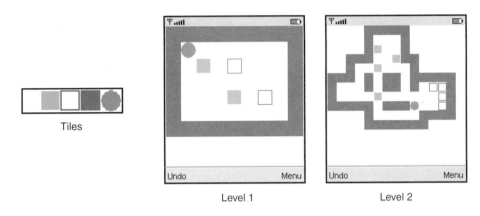

Figure 11.4 Different Tile Arrangements Form Different Game Layers

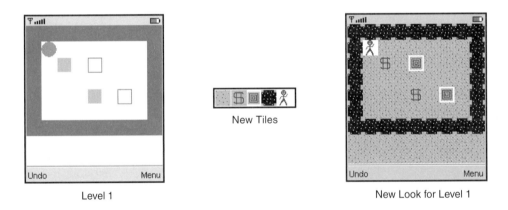

Figure 11.5 Different Tile Groups Form Different Themes

11.4   Layer Manager

A single screen can show multiple layers. For example, in Push Puzzle, the pusher is a simple tile, but it could be a sprite. If the pusher were a sprite, the screen would be made up of two layers: the background and the sprite. The game package includes a layer manager, which draws the individual layers onto the device screen.

11.4.1 Layer Ordering

The layer manager keeps the layers in an ordered list, and assigns the layers contiguous integers. The application developer can add and remove layers from the list. Layer zero is closest to the top; higher numbers are progressively further away.

MIDP Implementors

Strongly Recommend: If the application developer removes a layer from the middle of the list, renumber the remaining layers to keep them contiguous.

Strongly Recommend: Draw the layers onto the screen in order, beginning with the layers furthest from the user (the backgrounds) through the layer closest to the user (layer zero).

Application Developers

Strongly Recommend: Remember, when you use the layer manager, the order of your layers is important.

11.4.2 The View Window and Panning

The layer manager has a view window, which enables the application developer to choose which part of the layer is shown to the user. The ability to show only one part of a layer to the user at a time enables the application to use background panning. Figure 11.6 shows a game canvas using the view window; the user can see only part of the layer. The full canvas is shown in Figure 11.4, level two.

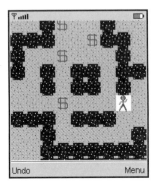

Figure 11.6   View Window Showing Part of a Game Canvas

Application Developers

 Strongly Recommend: As you consider whether to use panning, keep the input mechanism of the device in mind. A phone with a joystick-style disk is easier for users to pan with than a phone with only a keypad.

 Strongly Recommend: If you use a view window, make it as large as or smaller than the screen area being used. A view window that is larger than the visible screen may result in a computation that will not be used if the view window's content must be clipped to fit on the screen.

 Strongly Recommend: If you use a view window, keep the size of the display and the size of the image you are panning in proportion. A large image on a small display could be annoying to pan in certain games, especially those in which the user is expected to move quickly around the display. A large image on a small display could also be a problem in games that involve remembering the layout of the display. The game in Figure 11.6 is such a game. Users can easily lose the game if they forget the layout of walls. Forgetting is easier if most of the image is out of sight.

11.5   Performance and Resource Usage

This section has a few suggestions for improving the perceived performance of a game canvas. (See "Performance" on page 236 for general suggestions on improving the performance of a MIDP implementation and MIDlets.)

MIDP Implementors

Strongly Recommend: Because perceived performance is very important to games, use all available hardware capabilities to accelerate gaming content. The hardware capabilities that might be available on your device include hardware sprites, collision detection, tiling, and image compositing. Use a fast bitblit operation if it is available on your device.

Application Developers

Consider: When creating sprites, layers, and tiles for a game, consider creating the images then creating an indexed (256 color) super palette that averages all the colors from all the graphic components into a single palette. This reduces the palette required for the game, decreasing the memory footprint of the game.

11.6   Creating a Game

Application Developers

Consider: When you create a game, consider providing a Splash screen that can double as the Start screen. On this screen, give users access to instructions, and the ability to start and pause the game.

Recommend: With every game, provide a command of type HELP that displays a Help screen. Give the screen a label of Instructions and give the screen text that explain how to use your game. Be sure to document what behaviors you have mapped onto the game actions, if any.

Consider: When providing a Splash screen that can double as the Start screen, consider moving to this screen if the game is suspended. When the MIDlet restarts, consider giving the user the option to restart the game from the point it was suspended.

Consider: Creating a game using tiles and sprites is an art. The imagination and enthusiasm that you bring to the project will be reflected and transferred to those playing the game. This could result in a much more enjoyable user experience for everyone playing the game.

 Recommend: Always test your games on actual devices.

CHAPTER **12**

Abstract Commands

ABSTRACT commands enable application designers to define actions for a
MIDlet without specifying the accompanying user interface. Instead of requiring
application designers to put all actions on menus or buttons, MIDP implementors
decide how to present abstract commands. Giving this responsibility to MIDP
implementors makes MIDlets more portable. It also enables a MIDlet to be consistent with applications on a variety of devices, without porting any user-interface
code, and it increases the usability of your application because of tighter integration
with the device's native user interface.

An application can have any number of abstract commands. The commands
can be associated with a form item, a screen, or both. (See "Item-Specific Abstract
Commands" on page 88 and "Buttons and Hyperlinks" on page 97 for information
on commands associated with form items and how they can help to change the
look of strings and images.) The application developer can add or remove an
abstract command from a screen or an item as needed.

Application Developer Responsibilities	MIDP Implementor Responsibilities
• Text for short and long labels • Associated application action • Purpose (type) of the command • Importance (priority), compared to other abstract commands of the same type	• Mapping abstract commands to the device • Ordering of abstract commands • Label display policy (clipping or wrapping, when to use short or long label, when to show label) • Determining how user selects an abstract commands • Notifying the application when the user chooses an abstract command

An abstract command has three parts: a *command type*, a *label*, and a *priority*.
There are two kinds of labels, *short* and *long*. The short label is required; the long

label is optional. The application developer creates the abstract commands and cannot update the command type, label, or priority of the instance. The application developer can add and remove the abstract commands from displayables as needed. (See *Programming Wireless Devices with the Java™ 2 Platform, Micro Edition* [17] for information on the Command API.)

Application Developers

 Strongly Recommend: Do not change a displayable's abstract commands while it is visible, unless the change is in response to a user action. Making arbitrary changes while the user is interacting with a displayable is disorienting, but users understand context-sensitive screens that change in response to their actions.

12.1   Types of Abstract Commands

An abstract command's type is a hint to the MIDP implementation of the command's purpose. There are eight types of abstract commands: BACK, SCREEN, ITEM, OK, CANCEL, STOP, HELP, and EXIT. All can be associated with a displayable. Only type ITEM should be associated with a form item.

MIDP Implementors

 Recommend: Use the command-type hint to take advantage of any corresponding device policies. For example, one command type is BACK, and it typically causes an application to return to a previous state. Most phone designs have a policy regarding which button is used for this operation. MIDP implementations can use the command-type hint to take advantage of this policy.

12.1.1   The BACK Command Type

The BACK command type is designed to be used to return to a previous state in the application. A screen might have multiple commands of type BACK.

Application Developers

Strongly Recommend: Use the BACK command type for actions that return users to the previous screen, to the start of an action that involves multiple screens, or to the start of your MIDlet. (The example commands could have the labels Back, Start Over, and Home.) In other words, use the BACK command type to return the user to any previous location that makes sense in your application.

12.1.2   The SCREEN Command Type

The SCREEN command type is designed to be used for actions that affect the entire screen or application. A screen might have multiple commands of type SCREEN.

Application Developers

Strongly Recommend: Use the SCREEN command type for setting application preferences, moving to the next screen in an application, saving the contents of a text box, and other actions that are not associated with a single item or element on the screen. If a command is associated with a selected item or element, use the ITEM command type instead. (See page 170 for more information.)

12.1.3   The ITEM Command Type

The ITEM command type is designed to be used for actions that affect a single item or element on a screen. For example, item-specific abstract commands should use this command type. A screen might have multiple commands of type ITEM.

Strongly Recommend: Attach a command of type ITEM to the screen that contains the items when a command applies to each item on the screen. Attach a command of type ITEM to the item itself if it applies to only some of the items on the screen.

For example, consider a screen that displays a list of email messages as hyperlink string items (see "Buttons and Hyperlinks" on page 97 for information). Reading the selected message would best be thought of as an ITEM command, and, because the action is associated with every item in the list, the command of type ITEM should be associated with the screen. Viewing any attachment of the selected message would also best be thought of as an ITEM command. Because the action is associated with only some items (those that have attachments), it should be associated with the individual items. (See page 170 for more information.)

12.1.4   The OK Command Type

The OK command type is designed to be used to provide a positive response to a query. A screen typically has at most one command of type OK.

Application Developers

Recommend: Use a command of type OK on a confirmation alert screen. (See "Alerts" starting on page 125 for information.) Figure 12.1 shows an alert that asks the user to confirm buying a set of tickets. The response indicating that the tickets should be bought is an abstract command of type OK. The command has the label Buy.

Figure 12.1   Screen with OK and CANCEL Abstract Commands

12.1.5   The CANCEL Command Type

The CANCEL command is designed to be used to provide a negative response to a query. A screen typically has at most one command of type CANCEL.

Application Developers

Recommend: Use the CANCEL command type with a Confirmation Alert screen. (See "Alerts" starting on page 125 for information.) Figure 12.1 shows an alert that asks the user to confirm buying a set of tickets. The response indicating that the tickets should not be bought is an abstract command of type CANCEL. The command has the label Cancel.

12.1.6 The STOP Command Type

The STOP command is designed to be used to stop a process *other than* the entire MIDlet. (To stop the entire MIDlet, use a command of type EXIT.) A screen typically has at most one command of type STOP.

Application Developers

Recommend: Use the STOP command in conjunction with noninteractive gauges. (See "Gauges" on page 107 for more information.) For example, consider a MIDlet that accesses a web page. During the time that the MIDlet sends the request and waits for a reply, it should show a screen that gives the user feedback that the MIDlet is working. The feedback screen should at least have a noninteractive gauge and an abstract command of type STOP. If the user chooses the abstract command (for example, because getting the web page is taking too long), the command should immediately stop the download of the page.

12.1.7 The HELP Command Type

The HELP command type is designed to be used for tutorials, Help screens, and other information that assists the user. A screen might have multiple commands of type HELP.

Application Designers

Recommend: In addition to using the HELP command type for instructions and other help, use them for your applications' About boxes so that they show up in a consistent location from device to device.

12.1.8 The EXIT Command Type

The EXIT command type is designed to be used to enable the user to exit the MIDlet. (To stop a process that the MIDlet is performing without stopping the MIDlet itself, use a command of type STOP.) A screen typically has at most one command of type EXIT.

MIDP Implementors

> *Consider*: Give users a way to exit a MIDlet, in case an ill-designed or broken MIDlet does not give users a way to move from a screen. One way to do this is to add a command of type EXIT to each screen.

> *Strongly Recommend*: When the user exits the MIDlet, return to the device's main application screen. Usability studies have shown that exiting to an intermediate screen (for example, one where the user chooses a MIDlet from the current MIDlet's MIDlet suite) is confusing. (See "Launching and Exiting MIDlet Suites" on page 190 for more information.)

12.1.9 SCREEN Versus ITEM Command Types

It can sometimes be difficult to decide whether a particular command is of type SCREEN or ITEM. Some actions can be either ITEM or SCREEN command types, depending on their context. For example, consider reading messages in an email application. On a screen that listed email messages, reading the selected message would best be thought of as a command of type ITEM. On the other hand, a command that allows users to switch from another task (such as writing a message) to reading messages would be best thought of as command of type SCREEN. If the application made both actions available to the user, it should have two abstract commands: one of type ITEM and the other of type SCREEN. It would use the two commands on different screens.

12.2 Labels

A label is the part of the abstract command that a MIDP implementation might show to the user. For example, the label could appear on a soft button or be used as a menu item.

12.2.1 Label Size

An abstract command can have either one or two labels. That is, an application developer must supply a short label, and has the option of providing a long label.

Application Developers

 Recommend: Keep labels as short as possible to minimize the chance that they will be clipped. Make short labels one word long, and long labels two to three words long. For example, Figure 12.2 shows an abstract command with a short label of Account and a long label of Account Settings. The MIDP implementation uses the long label in the system menu and the short label for the soft button. It is also possible that a short and a long label will be the same. For example, a command might have the labels Back and Back.

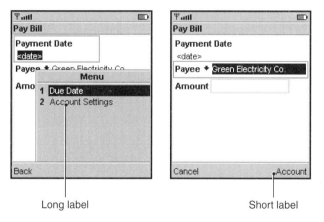

Long label   Short label

Figure 12.2   Abstract Command's Long and Short Labels

 Recommend: Always provide both a short and a long label. If an implementation has room for the long label, the usability of your application could be improved.

MIDP Implementors

 Strongly Recommend: If a command has both a long and a short label, try to use the long label. If it doesn't fit in the space available, use the short label. Note that you can use short labels for some commands and long labels for others. You can also switch between long and short labels. (This could be useful if, for example, the menu size changes.)

Consider: If your device uses a system menu, use the short label on soft buttons and the long label in the menu. Figure 12.2 shows this technique.

 Recommend: If a label is too long to be shown in the user interface, you are permitted to clip it. If you clip it, give users a visual indication; for example, an ellipsis is often used to indicate clipping.

 Strongly Recommend: Show at least four characters on the label of a soft button.

12.2.2   Label Text

Each command on a screen (no matter what its command type) should have a different label. If two commands have the same label, there will be no way for the user to distinguish one command from the other. For example, the MIDP Reference Implementation adds commands associated with an item to the system menu when the item has focus. If the item-specific command has the same label as a command associated with the screen, that label will appear twice on the system menu when the item has focus.

Note that a command's type and label are different. Users do not see a command's type; they see its label. A screen can have multiple commands of the same type. Figure 12.3 shows two commands of the same type with different labels.

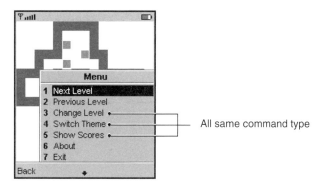

Figure 12.3 Abstract Commands of the Same Type with Different Labels

Application Developers

Consider: Make the first characters of labels unique so that users can tell one abstract command from another even if the labels are clipped.

Consider: Make your labels predictable so that the resulting action maps to the users' expectations for the label.

12.3   Priority

An abstract command's priority is an indication of the importance of an abstract command compared to other abstract commands of the *same type*.

Application Developers

 Recommend: One way to assign importance is to determine how often you expect a user to use the command. When assigning priorities, lower numbers indicate higher importance. For example, a command of priority 2 is more important than a command of priority 5. Priorities help MIDP implementations map commands to device capabilities, for example, making the higher-priority items easier to choose.

12.4   Implementing Abstract Commands

MIDP implementors determine the user interface for abstract commands so that their presentation and selection mechanisms can be appropriate for the device. Following device conventions enables MIDlets to conform to the native style of the device and feel natural to users.

MIDP Implementors

Strongly Recommend: Use device-appropriate mechanisms (such as soft buttons, hardware buttons, and menus) for your abstract command user interface. For example, if your device has "Go Back" operations on its right soft button, conform by placing a screen's highest-priority abstract command of type BACK on this button.

Strongly Recommend: Order commands from the application by type, and within type, by priority. Do not order commands by priority without regard to type. In the typical situation, where many command types have multiple commands, ordering by priority would be confusing to the user.

Strongly Recommend: If there is a command on a form item, let the user know by remapping the presentation of the abstract commands to include the item-specific abstract command. Make the item-specific command the most obvious one for the user. For example, place it first on a system menu.

Strongly Recommend: Determine and publish your algorithm for mapping abstract commands onto your device.

For example, a MIDP implementation for a mobile phone could use the following algorithm. (The algorithm is similar to the one used by the MIDP Reference Implementation.)

- Find any commands that map to hard buttons on the device, and assign them to those buttons.
  - The highest-priority command of type BACK maps to the Back hard button.
  - The highest-priority command of type EXIT maps to the End Call button (or

whichever button takes the user back to the Main screen of the device).

- Order the abstract commands by type in the following sequence: ITEM (associated with the item that has focus), ITEM (associated with the screen), SCREEN, and OK. These are abstract commands that users see as *positive* commands. Then order the rest of the commands by type in this sequence: HELP, BACK, CANCEL, STOP, and EXIT. These are abstract commands that users see as *negative* commands.

- Within type, order the abstract commands by priority, highest to lowest.

- Put the highest-priority negative command on one soft button, and the rest of the commands (positive followed by negative) on the other soft button. The MIDP Reference Implementation puts negative commands on the left, and positive commands on the right. Other devices might have other conventions.

   This algorithm gives users the ability to predict that negative commands are on one soft button, and positive commands are on the other. It is easily understood and accepted, even when the button the users consider positive has the extra negative commands at the bottom of its menu.

- If there is more than one command for the soft button that lists the rest of the commands, give that button a label of Menu and put the commands on a system menu. Figure 12.4 shows the system menu associated with the right soft button of a MIDlet.

Figure 12.4 System Menu

   The algorithm is useful for creating context-sensitive screens. If there are only item-specific commands on a screen, the command on the right system menu will change as the user traverses through the screen.

To illustrate the algorithm, assume that SmartTicket associates the abstract commands shown in Table 12.2 with the screen that has the user choose a movie. Further, assume that SmartTicket associates the abstract commands shown in Table 12.1 with the items on the screen.

Table 12.1: Abstract Commands for SmartTicket Items

Command Type	Priority	Long Label
ITEM	1	"Update Schedule" (associated with the Theater item)
ITEM	1	"Show Preview" (associated only with the movie item)

Table 12.2: Abstract Commands on a SmartTicket Screen

Command Type	Priority	Long Label
EXIT	5	"Exit SmartTicket"
HELP	1	"Help"
ITEM	2	"Change Theater"
SCREEN	1	"My Settings"
SCREEN	2	"Main Menu"

The user interface for SmartTicket on the mobile phone would then look like the screens in Figure 12.5; the system menu changes as the user navigates through the form.

Because each MIDP implementation will have its own algorithm, the user interface could look different on different devices. However, the benefit to users is that the presentation of abstract commands is integrated into the rest of the user interface on the device. Predictability is far more critical than having a consistent user interface across devices. (See "Make It Predictable" on page 9 for more information.)

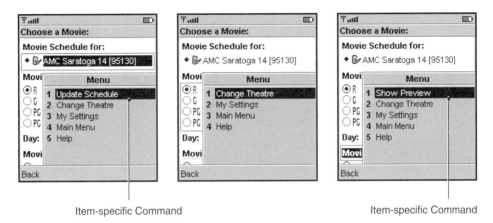

Item-specific Command   Item-specific Command

Figure 12.5 SmartTicket on a Mobile Phone

12.5 Using Abstract Commands

Actions that are not built into screen components (as dismissing is built into modal alerts), and are not low-level phone pad or game actions, are abstract commands. For example, abstract commands include actions such as restarting a game, selecting a movie from a list, or getting help.

Application Developers

> *Strongly Recommend*: Give each screen at least one command that en-
> ables the user to move to the next screen or to exit the application.

Although the MIDP specification permits an application to have screens without abstract commands, application developers should not create them. Such an application would be unusable; its users would be stuck on the screens that have no abstract commands.

MIDP Implementors

> *Recommend*: Give users a way to quit an application that has a screen
> without an abstract command. One way to do this is to add a command
> of type EXIT to each screen.

12.5.1　Determine the Abstract Commands for Each Screen

For example, SmartTicket is made up, in part, of the Splash screen, the screen that lists the high-level tasks users can do, and the screen for choosing a movie. The abstract commands associated with those screens are shown in Table 12.3.

Table 12.3: Screen Mock-ups and Abstract Commands

Sketch	Location in the Story	Abstract Commands
	At application launch	None The Splash screen is a timed alert.
	After the Splash screen (when the device owner already has an account)	• Exit the application • SELECT_COMMAND

Table 12.3: Screen Mock-ups and Abstract Commands (Continued)

Sketch	Location in the Story	Abstract Commands
Choose a Movie: ⊕ 12:20 pm ○ 2:30 pm ○ 4:45 pm ○ 7:00 pm ○ 9:15 pm *Seating prefer* *Number of tick* **menu** select seats show preview show by movies what's new? rate movies my settings about smartix cancel	If the user chooses "Show By Movie" command on the Movie-List screen	• Show a preview • Choose a movie by seeing a list of movies • See which movies will be coming soon • Update your account • See an About box • Update schedule (item specific) • See a preview (item specific) • Select seats (item specific)

Application Developers

Strongly Recommend: For each screen, select a type for each abstract command first, then prioritize the commands within each type. Resist the temptation to prioritize first. MIDP implementors map abstract commands by type, and consider priority a suggestion.

Consider: For each screen, ensure that commands of the same type have different priorities. Assigning commands the same type and priority does not help MIDP implementors with the layout of your abstract commands: commands with equal type and priority can appear in any order. The exception to giving every command associated with a screen a unique type/priority pair is *paired actions*—actions that work together, often to toggle some behavior. (See "Paired Commands" on page 181 for more information.)

For example, some MIDP implementors map the most important command within a type to a button, and place the rest on a menu. If multiple commands in a command type have top priority, then the MIDP implementor has no way to know which command to map to the button. Table 12.2 and Table 12.1 show the abstract commands associated with the Movie-Choosing screen of SmartTicket, and their priorities. Note that the two commands of type SCREEN have different priorities. Also note that the ITEM command for the screen is a lower priority than the item-specific commands. This ensures that if your MIDlet runs on a device that orders ITEM commands strictly by priority (instead of separately sorting item-specific and item commands, as recommended), your item-specific command will still appear more prominently.

12.5.2   Minimize Abstract Command Instances

Abstract commands can be used by multiple screens. The application would have less code, and possibly fewer maintenance issues, if screens that had the same abstract commands shared abstract command instances. For example, assume you have decided to update your MIDlet code to change the label of an abstract command present on several screens. If the screens all used the same abstract command instance, you would only have to change the code in one place.

Application Developers

> *Consider*: As you implement your application, use the same Command instance for abstract commands on different screens if they share the same type, label, and priority. Sharing commands across screens reduces the size of your application. This is an advantage unless sharing commands compromises your user-interface design.

If you would naturally give the commands on different screens different values, for example the same type and label but different priorities in relation to other commands of the same type, then create multiple Command instances. Note that it is not the absolute value of the command that is important, but its relationship to the other abstract commands of the same type on the screen.

12.5.3   Test on Multiple Devices

It is tempting, if an application is tested on a particular MID, to design for that layout. This can lead to problems because of the variation in MIDs' user interfaces.

Application Developers

> *Consider*: Test your MIDlets on multiple platforms to ensure that your application is usable and does not violate user-interface conventions.

Recommend: Become familiar with the user-interface conventions of common MIDs so that you can design and create applications that integrate cleanly into the native user interface of the device.

12.5.4 Paired Commands

Paired actions work together, often to toggle some behavior. The members of a paired action do not appear on the screen at the same time. For example, Pause and Resume are paired actions. When the user is running the application the Pause command would be available. If the user pauses the application, the Pause command would no longer be available; Resume would be available instead.

Ideally, when the user selects the visible command of a paired action, the other member of the pair would appear in the same place in the user interface. That is, one command of the pair should seem to take the place of the other. Figure 12.6 shows an example of a paired action in an older version of the Smart-Ticket application. Table 12.4 shows that the abstract commands in this paired action have the same type and priority.

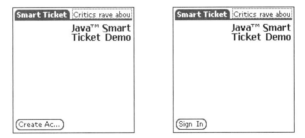

Figure 12.6 Paired Actions in an Earlier Version of SmartTicket

Application Developers

Recommend: To create a paired action, create two abstract commands that have different labels but the same types and priorities. You cannot create a single command and change its label because an abstract command is immutable: once created it cannot be changed. Immutable objects have a number of advantages, as detailed in *Effective Java™ Programming Language Guide (Java Series)* [15]. It also means that when you design a paired action, you create two abstract commands.

Recommend: Make sure that other commands on the paired action's screen, which have the same type as the paired action, have different priorities from it. This, in addition to giving the paired action's commands equal types and priorities, should enable MIDP implementors to replace one member of a paired action with the other.

For example, Table 12.4 shows that the priorities of the commands on the screen in Figure 12.6 have the same priority.

Table 12.4: Abstract Commands in SmartTicket, Organized by Screen

Screen	Abstract Command (Label: Description)	Type	Priority
Initial screen	Sign In: Sign in to the application, if account has been created	SCREEN	1
	Create Account: Create an account, only if this has not yet been done	SCREEN	1
	About SmartTicket: Display information about the application	HELP	2

CHAPTER 13

Application Discovery, Installation, and Management

A DEVICE must have a way for users to find and install new MIDlet suites, run MIDlet suites, remove old MIDlet suites, and so on. These tasks are called *application management*, and are the responsibility of the MIDP implementor. (See "Over the Air User-Initiated Provisioning Specification," which is part of the *MIDP 2.0 Specification* [19].)

Application designers cannot affect a device's application management but they can help users in other ways, such as taking care in naming their MIDlets and MIDlet suites. They must also supply information to the MIDP implementation that assists in application management.

13.1 Integrating MIDP into the Device

Underlying the decisions about how to implement application management tasks is the larger question of how to integrate MIDP into the device.

MIDP Implementors

Recommend: Integrate MIDP application management into the device's native application-management functionality. Have the device treat a MIDlet like a native application. Don't require users to start the Java platform on the device and then manage their MIDlets.

Although MIDP implementors might want to advertise their use of Java technology by having users launch the Java platform to manage MIDlets, using native application-management functionality provides more predictability. Users already know how to manage native applications, so there is no extra training required and fewer support issues. Because of the importance of predictability, using the native application-management functionality is more likely to be successful in the long run.

Sun's MIDP for Palm OS uses the native application-management functionality to manage MIDlets. As Figure 13.1 shows, MIDP for Palm OS places icons for MIDlet suites on the application launcher with native applications. Tapping the icon runs the application, whether the application is native or a MIDlet suite. Other management tasks, such as installing and removing applications, are also the same for native applications and MIDlet suites.

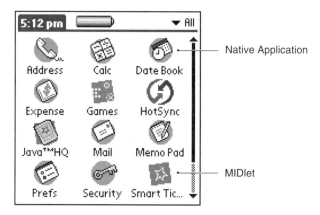

Figure 13.1   MIDlet and Native Application Icons on the Launcher

13.1.1 Icons

Many devices include icons in their Application Management screens. The icons help remind users what an application does. A MIDlet's icons can be supplied by either the MIDP implementor or the application developer.

MIDP Implementors

> *Consider*: Use the MIDlet suite's icons if they are present. If a MIDlet suite has an icon that is too large, consider top- and left-justifying it, then clipping it; if an icon is too small, consider centering it on a background of the correct size.

Recommend: Have generic icons for MIDlet suites and MIDlets. Use the generic icons if the MIDlet suite does not include icons, or includes icons that you cannot use. For example, the icon associated with SmartTicket, shown in Figure 13.1, is a generic icon for MIDlet suites that have only one MIDlet.

Application Developers

Consider: Provide 12-by-12 pixel, color icons in PNG format that devices can show to users. The icons should also look good displayed in grayscale. A MIDlet suite can contain one icon for the suite and one icon for each MIDlet.

Application developers provide icons by putting the PNG files into the MIDlet suite's JAR file, and by setting the values of the corresponding `MIDlet-Icon` and `MIDlet-n-Icon` properties. The properties can be in the MIDlet suite's JAD file or its JAR file's manifest. (See "Getting Information on MIDlet Suites" on page 194 for more information on the properties and values that can be in a MIDlet suite's JAD and JAR files.)

Recommend: If you provide an icon for a MIDlet suite that contains multiple MIDlets, the icon should graphically indicate it. For example, the Games MIDlet suite has multiple MIDlets. The icon for the Games MIDlet suite, shown in Figure 13.1, indicates this by having multiple items (such as the ball) that are meant to represent games.

13.1.2   Personal Storage for MIDlet Suites

Some operators give their users a personal storage area, which holds data that the user can download to their device. For example, some operators allow their users to use the area to store wallpaper or games that they have bought.

MIDP Implementors

Consider: Integrate MIDlet suites into the personal storage area, if the operator you are working with offers that service to its users. This would enable you to charge users only once for a particular version of a MIDlet suite, even if they have to reinstall it later. (That is, if they install it from their personal storage area, they would not be charged.) Users might have to download a MIDlet and install it a second time if, for example, the MIDlet became corrupted or they deleted it by mistake.

13.2   Discovering MIDlet Suites

The application that enables users to discover MIDlets is often a browser. Note, though, that the browser does not manage applications. Similarly, a MIDlet does not run in a browser; it is not an applet. The MIDP runtime launches and manages the life cycle of a MIDlet.

MIDP Implementors

Consider: Have the application used to discover MIDlets launch an installer if the user chooses to download a MIDlet. The browser should not do the installation.

 Recommend: Work with service providers to determine how users will find MIDlets to install or update. Possibilities include giving users a list of MIDlets available from the service provider (a *walled garden*), allowing users to choose among MIDlets from "approved" sites on the network, and so on. Figure 13.2 shows an example of a mobile phone that gives users a list of MIDlets to install or update and an example of an approved site to browse for MIDlets.

Figure 13.2   List of MIDlets That Users Can Install or Update

It will be easiest for users if they do not have to enter a URL, which can be tedious on a phone keypad. Instead, give users access to a list of MIDlets from the service provider, or a list of approved web sites from which to choose MIDlets, so that typically they do not have to enter a web address.

13.3 Installing MIDlet Suites

After users discover a MIDlet, they can choose to download it. The MIDP implementation handles the download and installation process, and should give users a chance to confirm that they want to install the MIDlet. If the MIDlet has a JAD file, the MIDP implementation should get information from it and display the information for the user during the confirmation request. The MIDP implementation should display at least the name, version, vendor, and size information, as shown in Figure 13.3.

Figure 13.3 Confirmation Screen before a MIDlet Installation

The application developer puts the MIDlet suite's name, version, vendor, and size into the JAD file. (See "Getting Information on MIDlet Suites" on page 194 for more information.)

Application Developers

 Recommend: Name your MIDlet suite and MIDlets so that users can tell what they contain. It can be difficult for users to remember what is in MIDlet suites with generic names like Demos and Examples. (Users will

also see the name when the MIDlet suite is on the device. For example, it could appear in a list of applications to launch or delete.)

Recommend: Make the first several characters of your MIDlet suite name unique. Your application will probably be in a list with other applications, and the user may only see the first several characters of your name. If your company name is at the beginning, and you have more than one application in the list, users will not be able to easily distinguish one of your applications from another. If you want to include your company name in the MIDlet suite name, put it at the end. For example, use "MyMidlet by MyCompany" instead of "MyCompany MyMIDlet."

MIDP Implementors

Strongly Recommend: Do not charge users for downloading a JAD file. After downloading the JAD file and using the information to create a confirmation dialog, the user might choose not to install the MIDlet. Instead, apply the charge when the user installs the MIDlet suite's JAR file.

Consider: If the user chooses to install a MIDlet suite already on the device, gracefully change from an installation to an update. For example, the MIDP Reference Implementation uses the message in the third screen of Figure 13.4 to ask the user whether to install a MIDlet suite when the device already has the same version installed. (See "Updating MIDlet Suites" on page 197 for more information updating MIDlet suites.)

Figure 13.4 Changing From Installation to Update of a MIDlet Suite

If the user decides to install the MIDlet suite, the MIDP implementation downloads the JAR file and proceeds with the installation.

 Recommend: Put an abstract command on the Installation screen to stop the download and installation of a MIDlet suite. If the user chooses the Stop command, revert the device to the state that it was in at the start of the installation procedure.

After the installation reaches a point where it cannot be stopped, remove the Stop command from the screen. For example, remove the command after the download of the JAD and JAR files has completed, and the device is finishing the installation locally. Figure 13.5 shows the screen used by the MIDP Reference Implementation.

Figure 13.5 Screen for Finishing an Installation

If the user decides not to use the MIDlet after the Stop command is taken off the screen, the user has to remove the MIDlet suite from the device instead of merely stopping the installation.

 Recommend: If you find a problem that keeps you from installing the MIDlet suite, give the user a clear error message. For example, tell the user if the device does not have enough memory, or the JAR file is corrupt, or there is a connection conflict with a static port registration. If possible, help the user solve the problem. For example, if there is not enough memory, you could show the user where memory is being used so that they have the option to free up space. Figure 13.6 shows an error message from the MIDP 2.0 Reference Implementation.

Figure 13.6 Error Message for a MIDlet Installation Problem

13.4 Launching and Exiting MIDlet Suites

This section assumes that the MIDP implementor is using the native launch mechanism on the device so that users launch MIDlets suites in the same way as they launch native applications. It also assumes that when the user exits a MIDlet suite, they are returned to the native operating environment, not to a special MIDP environment.

MIDP Implementors

Recommend: Present a MIDlet suite with only one MIDlet in a way that enables users to directly launch the MIDlet and to exit to the application launcher after they are through. When you represent the MIDlet, you show the icon associated with the MIDlet, as opposed to the one associated with the MIDlet suite.

For example, the SmartTicket MIDlet suite contains only one MIDlet. When this MIDlet suite is installed on a device running Sun's MIDP for Palm OS, tapping the SmartTicket icon starts the SmartTicket MIDlet, the only MIDlet in the suite. Figure 13.7 shows this sequence; when the user chooses the Smart Ticket icon from the screen on the left, SmarTicket launches and the screen on the right appears.

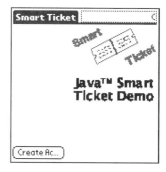

Figure 13.7 Single MIDlet Launched Immediately

 Recommend: Represent a MIDlet suite with multiple MIDlets so that users can choose a MIDlet from the suite after launching the suite (a MIDlet Chooser screen).

For example, the Games MIDlet suite contains multiple MIDlets. As Figure 13.8 shows, when this MIDlet suite is installed on a device running Sun's MIDP for Palm OS, tapping the Games icon shows users an interim screen that enables them to choose which MIDlet in the Games MIDlet suite they would like to launch.

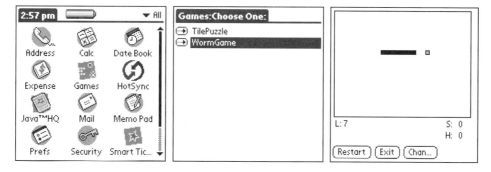

Figure 13.8 Launching a MIDlet through a MIDlet Chooser Screen

The MIDP 1.0 Reference Implementation, shown in Figure 13.9, took a different approach, which did not work as well in user testing. Its application launcher shows both MIDlet suites and MIDlets, and enables users to launch either. If a MIDlet suite has a single MIDlet, only the MIDlet is represented.

Figure 13.9 MIDP 1.0 Reference Implementation's Application Launcher

Users reported feeling confused because they didn't know what they were looking at. They thought that the item representing the MIDlet suite was a folder in a file system.

The MIDP 2.0 Reference Implementation, shown in Figure 13.10, now uses the same approach as Sun's MIDP for Palm OS. The application launcher shows the MIDlet suite and an interim screen if the suite has multiple MIDlets.

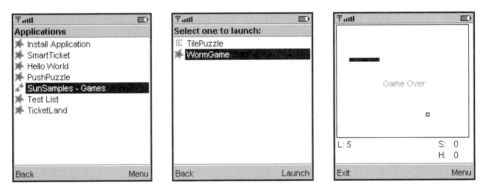

Figure 13.10 Application Launcher to MIDlet Chooser Screen

Sun's MIDP for Palm OS and the MIDP 2.0 Reference Implementation behave differently, however, when the user exits a MIDlet from a suite with multiple MIDlets. For example, in MIDP for Palm OS, if the user exited the WormGame MIDlet (which is a MIDlet in a suite of multiple MIDlets), the user was returned to the MIDlet Chooser screen.

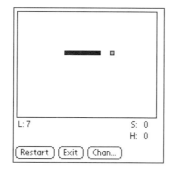 

Figure 13.11 Not Recommended: Return to the MIDlet Chooser Screen

The MIDP 2.0 Reference Implementation, shown in Figure 13.12, returns the user to the application launcher. In usability testing, users preferred this model. Whichever model you follow, check your design with usability tests to make sure users understand it.

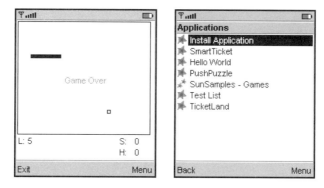

Figure 13.12 Return to the Application Launcher Screen

MIDP Implementors

Recommend: When the user exits a MIDlet that is part of a MIDlet suite with multiple MIDlets, exit to the application launcher (Figure 13.12), not a screen to choose a MIDlet in the suite. Usability testing has shown that users become confused if they are not returned to the application launcher.

13.5   Getting Information on MIDlet Suites

MIDP Implementors

Recommend: Give users a way to see information about a MIDlet suite, such as its version number, the names of its MIDlets, how much memory it is using, and so on. (See Chapter 15 for information on Security, and how to present it to the user.) For example, Figure 13.13 shows information about a MIDlet installed on a mobile phone.

Figure 13.13   Information about the Games MIDlet Suite

Recommend: If the device has a standard mechanism for giving users information about the native applications, leverage that mechanism for providing information about MIDlet suites. The *MIDP 2.0 Specification* [19] requires that you provide the version number, but you do not have to provide all the information shown in Figure 13.13. For example, Figure 13.13 shows Sun's MIDP for Palm OS, which uses the standard Palm OS Information screens, although it means that the names of the MIDlets in the suite are not listed.

Figure 13.14 Palm OS Information on the Games MIDlet Suite

13.5.1 JAD File Attributes

The Java application descriptor (JAD file) is one way that an application developer provides information to the MIDP implementation. The MIDP implementation presents the information in the JAD file to the user to confirm that the user wants to install the MIDlet suite. The JAD file can also hold information for the MIDlets themselves. (The manifest of the JAR file can also provide information. See "JAR File Attributes" on page 196.)

Application Developers

> *Strongly Recommend*: Provide a JAD file as part of your MIDlet suite package. A JAD file is optional but very useful to the MIDP implementation, especially during the installation process.

If a JAD file is present, it must contain the MIDlet suite's name, version, vendor, JAR file URL, and JAR file size. It is permitted to contain a number of other attributes, such as a description of the MIDlet suite, and security-related information. (See the *MIDP 2.0 Specification* [19] for a full list of attributes; see Chapter 15 for more information on MIDP 2.0 security.)

> *Consider*: If you provide a JAD file, consider including attributes that the MIDP implementation could provide to users to help them decide whether to use the MIDlet suite. For example, a description of the MIDlet, a URL where the user could get more information, and the names of the MIDlets in the MIDlet suite could be useful to the user.

MIDP Implementors

> *Consider*: Consider providing additional information, if it is present in the JAD file, that would help users decide whether to install the MIDlet suite. For example, if there is a description of the MIDlet suite, include that in the confirmation dialog.

There are three additional attributes that can only appear in a JAD file (if the application developer provides them at all). These attributes give the following pieces of information to the MIDP implementation:

- URL to use to report the new installation or the update of the MIDlet suite

- URL to use to report the deletion of the MIDlet suite

- Text message to show to the user when asking the user to confirm the deletion of the MIDlet suite

13.5.2   JAR File Attributes

The manifest of the MIDlet suite's Java archive (JAR) file is one way that an application developer provides information to the MIDP implementation. The manifest of the JAR file must contain the MIDlet suite's name, version, and vendor. It is also permitted to contain other information, such as the required J2ME™ profile, the registrations for MIDlets to handle inbound connections, MIDlet-specific information, and so on. The information is provided as a list of attribute-value pairs. (See the *MIDP 2.0 Specification* [19] for a full list of attributes.)

13.5.3   Interactions of Attributes in the JAD and JAR Files

If the MIDlet suite includes a JAD file, three attributes (the MIDlet suite's name, version, and vendor) must be present in both it and the JAR file's manifest. Their values must be identical or the device cannot install the MIDlet suite.

MIDP Implementors

> *Strongly Recommend*: If the application developer puts any other attributes in both files, and the MIDlet suite is trusted, the values of the attributes must be identical or you cannot install the MIDlet. If the MIDlet suite is untrusted, use the value from the JAD file.

Either the JAD file or the manifest of the JAR file must contain the required J2ME platform configuration and profile, as well as the name, class name, and optionally the icon for each MIDlet in the suite.

13.6   Updating MIDlet Suites

When a user requests the installation of a MIDlet that is already on the device, the device should treat this as a request to update the MIDlet suite. (If the version of the requested MIDlet suite is the same as the version on the device, this can also be called *reinstalling*. From the device perspective, though, it is an update.)

MIDP Implementors

Strongly Recommend: Before you perform the update, the user must confirm the operation. In the screen that requests confirmation, tell the user whether the requested MIDlet suite is older, newer, or the same as the version on the device. Figure 13.15 shows a Confirmation screen from the MIDP 2.0 Reference Implementation.

Figure 13.15 Confirmation Screen for Updating a MIDlet Suite

MIDP implementations should not charge users for reinstalling a MIDlet suite after they have paid for it. They might be reinstalling it because they deleted it by mistake, or because it was corrupted on their device. In either case, they have already paid for the use of that version of the MIDlet suite. (See "Personal Storage for MIDlet Suites" on page 185 for one way that the user could reinstall a MIDlet suite without being charged.)

13.6.1 Security

MIDP Implementors

 Strongly Recommend: If the MIDlet suite being updated had a digital signature to show that it was from a trusted entity and had not been tampered with, you must not permit the user to update it with an unsigned MIDlet suite.

If the MIDlet suite being updated included protected functionality, the new MIDlet should use the same permission levels.

13.6.2 Application Data

MIDP Implementors

 Strongly Recommend: If the MIDlets from the MIDlet suite being updated have saved data on the device, make it available to the updated MIDlet suite if it is identical to the existing MIDlet suite, or if its JAR or JAD file is from the same location as the one for the existing MIDlet suite.

If the updated MIDlet suite is not identical or from the same location as the existing MIDlet suite, ask the user whether to keep the data. Figure 13.16 shows a screen that queries the user.

Figure 13.16 Confirmation Screen for Saving a MIDlet Suite's Data

13.7 Removing MIDlet Suites

Users must remove an entire MIDlet suite; MIDlets cannot be removed from their MIDlet suites.

MIDP Implementors

 Recommend: Confirm that users want to remove a MIDlet suite before deleting it from the device. Tell them what is in the suite, and that removing the suite also removes its associated data. Figure 13.17 shows the relevant screen in the MIDP 2.0 Reference Implementation.

Figure 13.17 Confirmation Screen for Removing a MIDlet Suite

If the MIDlet suite's JAD file included a text message to show to users being asked to confirm the deletion of the MIDlet suite, include it on the Confirmation screen. (The message is the value of the `MIDlet-Delete-Confirm` attribute.) In Figure 13.18, the `MIDlet-Delete-Confirm` attribute contained the string, "Push-Puzzle is a really cool app, and should not be removed."

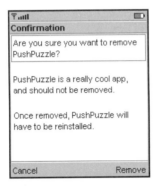

Figure 13.18 Confirmation Screen with the Text Message from the JAD File

MIDP Implementors

Recommend: If the device has a standard mechanism for removing native applications, leverage that mechanism for MIDlet suites. For example, Sun's MIDP for Palm OS, shown in Figure 13.19, uses the standard Palm OS application deletion functionality, although it means that the contents of the MIDlet suite are not listed.

Figure 13.19 Deleting a MIDlet Suite From a Palm OS Device

13.8   Handling Application Management Errors

The *MIDP 2.0 Specification* [19] mandates that the user be informed of certain application management errors. In other cases, a MIDP implementation should only inform the user of critical errors. This applies the advice, "Minimize Interruptions From MIDP and MIDlets" on page 13.

MIDP Implementors

Strongly Recommend: When you tell users about a problem, provide error messages that they can understand and, if appropriate, can act on in order to fix the problem. Useful error messages include the following information:

- What's wrong; for example, "The server cannot accept your request at this time."
- Why it's wrong, if you know and can tell them in a meaningful way; for example, "This could happen if the system is too busy."
- What to do about it; for example, "Try again later."

Make a distinction between a problem with the device (such as a low battery), with the server (such as an unavailable JAR file), with the connection (such as a dropped connection), and with data transmission (such as getting corrupt data).

Figure 13.20 shows an example of a good error message.

Figure 13.20 Good Error Message

Figure 13.21 shows examples of poor error messages. The error message on the left is too terse. It tells the user what the problem is, but it doesn't tell the user why the problem might have occurred or what to do about it. The error message on the right has the same problem, and in addition, it does not tell the user what problem occurred.

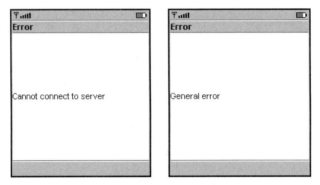

Figure 13.21 Not Recommended: Poor Error Messages

CHAPTER 14

Push Functionality

THE *MIDP 2.0 Specification* provides *push functionality*, which enables a device to automatically launch a MIDlet to handle an incoming message. Examples of potential push-enabled MIDlets include news services, concert information, and so on.

Application Developer Responsibilities	MIDP Implementor Responsibilities
• Statically registering required connections • Dynamically registering connections that your MIDlet can use but that are not required • Handling all I/O for the running MIDlet • Handling any time-based functionality in your MIDlet while it is running	• Determining which protocols will be used • Maintaining a list of connections, alarms, and associated data (such as which entities may send messages) • Permitting only one registration for each connection • Listening for inbound connection notifications • Getting permission to interrupt and to launch a MIDlet • Launching a MIDlet to handle an incoming message • Launching a MIDlet in response to an alarm • Giving the MIDlet any data buffered from the message

Application Developers

Strongly Recommend: Push functionality launches a MIDlet. It is not responsible for notifying a running application that a message has arrived for it. You must ensure that your MIDlet can handle its own I/O once it is running.

Push functionality requires that the user give permission to automatically start the MIDlet. This is because launching a push-enabled MIDlet may require the currently running MIDlet to exit.

MIDP Implementors

Strongly Recommend: The user controls the interruption behavior of a MIDlet that uses push functionality. Give users a range of options, from prohibiting a MIDlet from receiving push messages to receiving all of its messages without asking for further permission. Figure 14.1 shows the options available to the user in the MIDP Reference Implementation. (See "Security" starting on page 211 for more information.)

Figure 14.1   Options for Handling Pushed Messages

Consider: In addition to the options shown in Figure 14.1, consider giving users the option to allow an interruption only when there is no application running. This would enable the user to disallow interrupts to running MIDlets without completely turning off the push functionality.

14.1   Registering to Use Push Functionality

To receive messages, a MIDlet must register with the device to give it connection end points from which it might receive messages and from whom it will accept messages. A connection end point specification includes the protocol, host (optionally), and port number.

When there is an incoming message from an acceptable entity, the device launches the registered MIDlet. Note that push functionality should not allow the device to receive arbitrary messages from any entity. The application that registers to use the push functionality specifies which entities are permitted to send messages; that specification is called a *filter*. In other words, push functionality does not require the device to accept all unsolicited messages; it does not make the user of a device vulnerable to spam.

Note that push functionality might be blocked temporarily during the installation and deletion of a MIDlet suite.

Application Developers

 Strongly Recommend: If your MIDlet must be able to use a particular connection to receive messages in order to function correctly, declare this in the MIDlet suite's JAD file.

Declaring your push requirements in the JAD file is called *static* registration. If your MIDlet can operate without receiving pushed messages, or does not require a well-known end point, register to use the port functionality from within the MIDlet. If possible, allow the device to allocate the port number. Registering to use push functionality from within the MIDlet is called *dynamic* registration.

MIDP Implementors

 Strongly Recommend: Only allow one push registration per connection end point. If a user tries to install a MIDlet suite that requests a connection end point that is already registered by another MIDlet, do not install the new MIDlet suite. If an installed MIDlet tries to dynamically register for a connection end point that is already registered by another MIDlet, do not accept the new registration.

 Strongly Recommend: If you cannot install a MIDlet due to a conflict in connections, provide clear error messages to the user to explain the problem. Figure 14.2 shows an error message from the MIDP Reference Implementation.

Figure 14.2   Error Message Reporting a Connection Conflict

MIDP Implementors, Continued

> *Consider*: Provide more information on the push registry and its entries in an advanced area. The information could be valuable for support purposes.

14.2   Use Cases for Push Functionality

Many types of applications can benefit from push functionality. For example, games that require users to take turns, such as chess, could be written using push. Because one turn can take a long time, when one player takes a turn, that turn could be pushed to the other player. The other player can then make a move, that move would be pushed, and so on.

Other examples are business applications that involve getting approvals from multiple people, especially when those approvals must be done in a certain sequence. Consider an expense report MIDlet. The application would push a request for approval to the first person. When the first person approves the report it is pushed to the second person, and so on. The report can be pushed back to the initiator if anyone declines to give their approval, or at the end of a successful approval process.

Push functionality is useful to applications for which data updates are intermittently available, such as a commuter's helper that could receive weather and travel advisories. Figure 14.3 shows another example, News Hound's news headline service. The service uses push functionality to provide interested users with a list of headlines of breaking news.

Figure 14.3 News Hound Using Push Functionality

Requests for help could also be written using push functionality. For example, consider a group of service technicians at customer sites. A technician having a problem could send a request for assistance to the group (in other words, it could be multicast). The technician could then accept the first offer of assistance.

Finally, some MIDlet suites that are downloaded as demos could use push to register the suite and upgrade it to full functionality. The demo MIDlet would dynamically register the push connection. When the demo MIDlet received the receipt and key, it could make its full functionality available and unregister the connection.

14.3 Protocols for Push Functionality

Some protocols are better suited to push technology than others. For example, short message service (SMS) is a store-and-forward protocol. A service center stores messages until they are fetched by the device. The device typically has a small *inbox* (cache of messages). If its inbox is full, a device's messages stay on the server. By contrast, datagram and socket are protocols that require that their messages be accepted immediately. There is a better chance that the message will get to the phone with the SMS protocol.

MIDP Implementors

Consider: Decide which network protocols you will make available for push applications on the device. Even if your device supports a protocol that accepts messages (for example, server sockets), you do not have to use that protocol to launch a MIDlet.

Application Developers

Consider: The network protocols available for push technology depend on the vendors. For example, some vendors support SMS while others might not. Similarly, some support socket connections but not datagrams, while others support datagrams but not sockets. Network protocols, or their cost, might also depend on the user's location. Some vendors might change which network services are available to users, or their pricing, when users are *roaming* (out of their local coverage area).

Contact the network operators for which you will be writing your MIDlet for details about the protocols they support for push functionality.

A device's choice of protocol also affects how an entity pushing a message addresses a device. With Internet Protocols (IP), most devices use the Dynamic Host Configuration Protocol (DHCP). Every time the user turns on the device, the device is assigned a new address. Any application that pushes a message either needs an operator's cooperation to get a message to the device (because the operator knows the IP address that the device is currently assigned) or the application has to register with entities that might push it data any time it gets a new IP address. In contrast, SMS messages use a well-known address to get a message to its recipient.

 Recommend: If you are not developing applications with a particular operator's cooperation, and are using an IP-based protocol, create a subscription mechanism for your application. Have the MIDlet register every time the user starts the device so that you can contact it when you need to push it data.

14.4   Alarms

In addition to enabling an application to be launched in response to an incoming message, push functionality enables a MIDlet to be launched at a particular time. This *alarm* functionality does not take the place of the timers that have been available since MIDP 1.0; they are meant to work together.

Application Developers

 Strongly Recommend: Use an alarm so that your MIDlet will be launched at a particular time; use a timer so that your MIDlet will take an action when it is running.

The device uses an alarm to start your MIDlet if the MIDlet is not running at a particular time of day; the alarm does not affect your MIDlet if it is already running. For a running MIDlet to take an action at a particular time, it must use a timer.

14.5   Designing a MIDlet Suite That Uses Push Functionality

Two concerns in the design of a MIDlet suite that uses push functionality are portability and ease of maintenance.

14.5.1   Portability

Devices have different resource limitations. Some devices might limit the number of available connections.

Application Developers

Consider: For portability, design your MIDlet suite to use only one connection at a time.

14.5.2   Ease of Maintenance

MIDlets in a suite can share push connections. Further, when a connection is registered, it can designate which MIDlet in the suite is run when that connection receives a message. These features enable a MIDlet suite to concentrate the push registration in one MIDlet of a MIDlet suite.

The scenario for the MIDlet suite would be as follows. One MIDlet would register all of the connection end points that the MIDlets in the suite will need. As part of each registration, it would specify which MIDlet in the suite to launch to handle pushed data. When a message is received, the push functionality would launch the appropriate MIDlet. The launched MIDlet would obtain a list of the connections for the MIDlet suite that have a message available and handle the incoming data.

Application Developers

> *Consider*: For ease of maintenance, consider concentrating push registration in one MIDlet of your MIDlet suite.

CHAPTER 15

Security

THE *MIDP 1.0 Specification* had a *sandbox* model for security. A sandbox model provides a MIDlet with a restricted set of APIs. These APIs do not provide access to any native functionality, nor to any functionality that might be security-sensitive.

The *MIDP 2.0 Specification* [19] introduces the concept of a *trusted* MIDlet suite: one or more MIDlets in a JAR file that has not been tampered with and was obtained from a trustworthy source. A trusted MIDlet suite can be given permission to use *protected* or *security-sensitive* APIs (APIs which might cost the user money or impact the user's privacy). In contrast, MIDlet suites that are *untrusted* (that is, MIDlet suites for which trust cannot be established) are either not permitted to access security-sensitive APIs, or are allowed only with explicit permission from the user.

This chapter covers the security concepts introduced in MIDP 2.0 and their impact on the user experience.

Application Developer Responsibilities	MIDP Implementor Responsibilities
• Listing in the JAD file the MIDlet's required protected APIs • Listing in the JAD the MIDlet's requested (but not required) protected APIs • Meeting the manufacturer or service provider's requirements for trusting the MIDlet suite • Being cognizant of prompts that result from using protected APIs	• Creating a security policy for the device, including protection domains, permissions, and so on • Protecting security policy and protection domain information on the device • Providing prompts to the user for authorizing MIDlet suites and MIDlets • Providing Help screens • Providing a way to update security settings

There are several places where the MIDP 2.0 security model impacts the user experience. Most of the impact is from untrusted MIDlet suites: Users must be informed when they are installing untrusted MIDlet suites; users must be prompted when a MIDlet tries to use a protected API for which it does not have permission (although even trusted MIDlet suites might require user permission for some behaviors); and users must be given a way to change the permissions on a MIDlet suite in an intuitive, easy-to-understand way.

Creating a good user experience can be difficult because consumers frequently do not understand security. Without a well-designed user interface, they might stop using an application due to ignorance or confusion rather than because they no longer need or want it.

MIDP Implementors

Recommend: Consider providing a Help screen everywhere security information or a trust indicator is shown. (See "Onscreen Indicators" on page 36 for information on trust indicators.) Figure 15.1 shows an example of a Help screen for security settings.

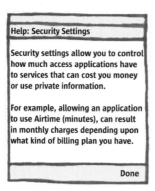

Figure 15.1   Help Screen for Security Information

15.1   Determining Trust

The idea of a trusted MIDlet suite implies that untrusted MIDlet suites might also be available to be installed on the device. MIDP implementations need to determine whether a MIDlet is trusted or untrusted.

MIDP Implementors

Recommend: Work with operators to decide how your MIDP implementation will determine whether a MIDlet suite is trusted. For example, you might use X.509 PKI, as described in the *MIDP 2.0 Specification* [19], or perhaps only MIDlets from the operator's web site will be trusted, and so on.

Because the MIDP 1.0 and MIDP 2.0 security models differ (for example, X.509 PKI was not part of the MIDP 1.0 security model, so those MIDlet suites would not be signed), MIDP 2.0 implementations need to fit MIDP 1.0 applications into their security models. The implementations must be able to run MIDP 1.0 MIDlet suites as untrusted applications.

Strongly Recommend: Your MIDP implementation must be able to run MIDP 1.0 MIDlets as untrusted applications

15.2   Working with a Security Policy

The level of trust in a MIDlet suite is determined by the *security policy* on the device. A security policy associates MIDlet suites with *protection domains*. Each MIDlet suite belongs to one, and only one, protection domain.

Protection domains list the protected APIs or functions that the device may allow the associated MIDlet suites to access. Protection domains also specify the maximum amount of access to the protected functions that its MIDlet suites can be given. For example, the protection domain could specify that its MIDlet suites will be granted access to some protected services only after getting approval from the user.

A device will most likely have at least two protection domains: trusted and untrusted. However, there may be more domains. For example, an operator domain may be required to allow the operator to install trusted MIDlets associated with their service. Domains can be created for other classes of applications as well.

MIDP Implementors

Recommend: Work with operators to create a set of protection domains.

Strongly Recommend: Protect the security policy and protection domain information on the device so that unauthorized entities cannot see or change it.

15.2.1 Permissions

A protection domain lists the protected APIs or functions to which it might grant access by listing the corresponding *permissions*. If a permission does not appear in a protection domain, then the MIDlet suites associated with the domain are denied access to those protected functions.

The name of a permission indicates the API or function it is protecting. For example, the name of the permission associated with the HTTP protocol is `javax.microedition.io.Connector.http`. (See the *MIDP 2.0 Specification* [19] for a list of the permissions it defines.)

Devices with advanced capabilities, such as multimedia recording or certain kinds of messaging, may have additional protected APIs, and therefore additional permissions. For example, the ability to record audio or video data may be protected.

MIDP Implementors

Strongly Recommend: Use your security policy to appropriately restrict access to protected APIs.

Note that not all APIs are protected. The *MIDP 2.0 Specification* identifies APIs that MIDlets must be able to run freely, without requiring permission from the user. These include APIs such as the user-interface and game functionality. (See the *MIDP 2.0 Specification* [19] for the full list.)

15.2.2 Permissions and Interaction Modes

In addition to permissions, a protection domain specifies the maximum amount of access to protected functions that a MIDlet in its domain can be granted. If the MIDlets can use the functionality without getting explicit user permission, they have an allowed permission-type. If the MIDlets must get explicit user permission before using the functionality, they have a user permission-type. The user permission type is further divided into *interaction modes*. The *MIDP 2.0 Specification* [19] defines these permissions and interaction modes:

- *Allowed permission*: MIDlet suites in the protection domain can use the API or function without involving the user. The name for this interaction mode is `Allowed`.

- *User permission*: MIDlet suites in the protection domain can use the API or function only after the user explicitly grants permission. The user is asked for permission when the MIDlet attempts to use the protected API. If the user denies permission, the MIDlet cannot make calls to the protected interfaces. Users can grant permission with one of the following interaction modes:

  - `Blanket`: Permission is granted for every invocation of the API by a MIDlet suite until it is uninstalled or the user changes the permission.

  - `Session`: The user is prompted when the MIDlet first attempts to use the protected API. If the user then grants permission, permission is granted until the user exits the MIDlet suite. If the user restarts the MIDlet suite, the permission request is repeated the first time the MIDlet attempts to access the protected API.

  - `Oneshot`: Permission is granted for one and only one immediately preceding function call. Each time the MIDlet calls the protected API, the permission request is repeated.

In addition to these interaction modes, users must be given the opportunity to deny permission when they are prompted.

MIDP Implementors

 Recommend: Work with operators to determine which permissions and interaction modes a protection domain should contain. For example, permissions in an operator domain may have only the allowed interaction mode, and permissions in the untrusted domain may have only the user interaction modes.

 Recommend: Limit your use of the Oneshot interaction mode. When users have to be interrupted before every single call to a protected function, they can become very impatient.

 Strongly Recommend: The *MIDP 2.0 Specification* [19] requires that an untrusted MIDlet be allowed to use the HTTP and HTTPS protocols if the user gives permission. That is, the untrusted domain must give a user interaction mode to the permissions for HTTP and HTTPS.

Application Developers

 Recommend: If your MIDlet is untrusted and uses protected functions, consider how often you are accessing those APIs. In certain situations, the number of prompts that the user is given could become very annoying. For example, if the permission level is set to oneshot, every access will result in a prompt to the user to ask permission to use that protected interface.

15.3   Function Groups: Permissions in a Usable Interface

MIDP implementations with security policies that incorporate more than one permission domain are likely to have long lists of protected APIs. If a prompt had to be presented for every permission, consumers would be overwhelmed and probably confused. They would not be likely to use that device or service again.

Extensive user studies on the use of certificates and security in web browsers have shown that most users have little patience for reading long tomes explaining why they need to approve a security request. They are also easily confused by the technical terms used, the many dialogs that can appear, and so on. These problems are compounded when the device being targeted has a small display and has different primary tasks than a browser.

The *function groups* model can be used to simplify permission requests. Function groups were first proposed in the *Recommended Security Policy for GSM/ UMTS Compliant Devices*, which is an addendum to the *MIDP 2.0 Specification* [19]. (Note that because security is an evolving area, this addendum is only a recommended practice, not a specification requirement.)

Function groups simplify the presentation of permissions by creating sets of related permissions. The user then interacts with the function group instead of with individual permissions. Any time a user changes the permission level for the function group, it affects all of the group's individual permissions.

 Strongly Recommend: Use function groups in your user interface— during installation, in user prompts (runtime security warnings and security errors), and when the user can set permission levels. In other words, use them where ever the user will encounter security.

The following list is the minimum recommended set of function groups, which set covers most of the basic functions expected to be on MIDP 2.0 devices:

- *Network- and cost-related groups*:
    - *Net Access*: permissions for functions that result in an active network data connection
    - *Messaging*: permissions for functions that allow sending or receiving messages
    - *Application Auto-Invocation*: permissions for functions that allow a MIDlet to be invoked automatically by the push or alarm functionality
    - *Local Connectivity*: permissions for functions that activate a local port to establish a connection
- *Privacy-related groups*: This covers multimedia recording, which represents permissions for functions that capture still images, tape video, or record audio clips.

MIDP Implementors

 Strongly Recommend: Whenever the user is shown a prompt or permission request, instead of showing them the actual API call or using a technical term, consider using a function group to present the concept. Use terms familiar to the user.

For example, the Network Access function group could be referred to as airtime. The user could then be asked if they are willing to give a MIDlet permission to use airtime. *Airtime*, in the United States, is the common term used by carriers to refer to the minutes the user pays for. The text of the permission request should reinforce any potential side effects like cost. Figure 15.2 shows a mock-up of a request.

Figure 15.2 Permission Request for the User

Instead of being confusing to the user, having the permission request use the common term "airtime" reminds the user that granting permission to the MIDlet could result in charges on their next bill. In addition, because the user grants the MIDlet permission to access functionality in the function group, the number of permission prompts might also be reduced. (For example, the user would not have to grant separate permissions for the MIDlet to use HTTP and HTTPS if they were both in the Network Access function group.)

15.4   Installing a MIDlet Suite

One of the first places a user encounters security issues is during MIDlet suite installation. At a minimum, the user should always be presented with the trust level of the MIDlet suite before the suite is installed, as shown in Figure 15.3. In addition, the MIDlet must be assigned to a protection domain and, depending on the needs of the MIDlet suite and the protection domain's permissions, the user may be asked to grant permissions during the installation.

15.4.1 Communicating a MIDlet Suite's Level of Trust

A user should be asked for confirmation before a MIDlet suite is installed. This would typically be done after the JAD file is downloaded but before the JAR file is downloaded. In MIDP 2.0, the Confirmation screen should also include any information on the trust level of the MIDlet suite. One place that trust information can be found is in any certificate used to sign the MIDlet suite. Figure 15.3 shows a mock-up of a Confirmation screen with some security information.

Figure 15.3   Trust Level on Confirmation Screen during Installation

MIDP Implementors

 Strongly Recommend: Include information about the trust level of the MIDlet suite in the Installation Confirmation screen. Users should know what they are installing *before* they install it.

Consider: If the MIDlet suite is signed, include relevant information from the certificate, such as its organization, country, and subject.

 Strongly Recommend: If the MIDlet suite being installed is updating an existing MIDlet, and the existing MIDlet had a digital signature, the installation can only continue if the new MIDlet suite is also signed.

15.4.2 Authenticating a MIDlet under a Protection Domain

During installation, a MIDlet suite *authenticates under* a particular protection domain. That is, each protection domain has a different entry criterion. One protection domain might be for MIDlets signed by a particular entity, another might be for

MIDlets from a particular web site, and so on. A MIDlet that meets the entry criterion for a domain is said to authenticate under that protection domain. MIDlets that cannot authenticate under any of the device's trusted protection domains (but have no other problems with their MIDlet suite packaging and could otherwise be installed) are assigned to the untrusted protection domain.

MIDP Implementors

Recommend: Work with operators to ensure that your implementation authenticates MIDlet suites under the correct protection domains. For example, an operator may want MIDlet suites signed by different entities to be authenticated under different domains, or may want MIDlet suites on its portal to authenticate under a particular domain, and so on.

Protection domains may not be an issue for MIDlet suites that do not use protected functions. These MIDlet suites can run in the same way whether they are in a trusted or an untrusted domain. Other MIDlet suites, though, must be installed in a domain that can grant them access to the protected functions they require.

Application Developers

Recommend: If your MIDlet suite requires protected functions, ask operators and MIDP implementors how to get your MIDlet suite onto their devices in a trusted domain. For example, you might be able to get your MIDlet suite shipped with the device, or made available from the operator's portal. You might have to have the MIDlet signed by a certain entity so that the MIDlet can be installed on the device.

15.4.3 Authorization

Trying to grant permissions, whether by the device or the user, is called *authorization*. If permission is granted, it is a successful authorization. One of the times that a MIDlet suite is authorized is during installation. If the authorization is not successful, the MIDlet cannot be installed.

Authorization during the installation process occurs after the MIDlet suite is authenticated under a domain. The MIDP implementation can then check the permissions requested by the MIDlet suite against the permissions that the protection domain could grant.

So that it can be authorized, a MIDlet suite should specify its needs for protected APIs in its JAR manifest or JAD file. (See *Programming Wireless Devices with the Java™ 2 Platform, Micro Edition* [17] for more information on these files.) In these files, a MIDlet suite can specify that certain permissions are required and that others, while nice to have, are not required.

Application Developers

Strongly Recommend: Specify that a permission is required if your MIDlet cannot function without it. For example, if your MIDlet enables users to browse an online catalog, it couldn't function without HTTP. Specify that a permission is nice to have, but not required, if your MIDlet can operate with or without it. (The functionality available without the permission is permitted to be at a lower level than if the permission were granted.) For example, if your MIDlet is a game that allows its users to save their scores on a server, users could still play the game without using HTTP; they just couldn't publish their scores.

MIDP Implementors

Strongly Recommend: If the MIDlet suite requires a permission that your security policy cannot grant, do not install the MIDlet suite. If the MIDlet suite requests, but does not require, permissions that the device cannot grant, continue installing the MIDlet suite.

Recommend: If a MIDlet suite cannot be installed because it is untrusted and it requires protected functions, display a message that explains the situation in user-friendly terms, as the message in Figure 15.4 does.

Figure 15.4   Untrusted MIDlet Suite Requiring Protected Functions

15.5   Prompting the User for Permission

When a MIDlet tries to call a protected API, use protected functions, or, in some cases, be automatically launched, the MIDP implementation checks whether the MIDlet has been granted permission. If it must, the MIDP implementation queries the user about whether to grant the permission. If the MIDlet is successfully authorized, the MIDP implementation runs the protected code. If the MIDlet has not been granted access, the MIDP implementation throws a `SecurityException`. (See *Programming Wireless Devices with the Java™ 2 Platform, Micro Edition* [17] for information on the exception.)

Permissions that have user interaction levels can cause the MIDP implementation to query the user. For example, if the MIDlet is running and the user has set the permission's interaction level to `oneshot`, the MIDP implementation will have to ask the user for permission to run the protected function. Querying the user for permission should ask only one straightforward question and use every-day language.

MIDP Implementors

 Strongly Recommend: Keep the permission request simple and straightforward: ask users only for permission. Do not combine the permission request with other tasks, such as changing the MIDlet's interaction level. With the simple request, such as the one shown in Figure 15.5, a reply of Yes means they grant permission, No means they deny permission.

Figure 15.5   Straightforward, Yes-or-No Permission Request

Asking for permission assumes the user can understand the prompt and make an intelligent decision. It also assumes that the user has some knowledge about security concepts, which is not necessarily a valid assumption to make. Don't compound the complexity by asking even more of the user.

If your implementation tries to do more than ask for permission, for example by also offering the ability to change the interaction level, the interaction will not be simple and straightforward. Users will not be able to get through the runtime warning as quickly, and could become seriously confused. In user studies on the MIDP 2.0 Reference Implementation where permission level options were combined with the permission question, some consumers were unable to figure out what to do. (Figure 15.6 shows a mock-up of such a screen.) The result was a security nightmare—in some cases, users just selected anything and did not understand the implications of their choice. They just wanted the prompt to go away.

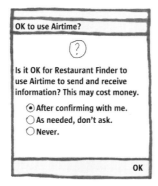

Figure 15.6   Not Recommended: Combined Permission Request and Level-Setting

Instead of combining the permission request with the ability to set the permission level, have the user do the two tasks separately. Make sure the user has access to a security-settings user interface where permission levels can be presented in a more understandable and less stressful context. Figure 15.7 shows screens that provide such settings.

MIDP Implementors

Strongly Recommend: If you do decide to allow users to change or set permissions as part of a permissions prompt, as well as with a security-setting user interface, synchronize the two user interfaces. Have them use similar words and, if the user changes or sets the interaction level with one method, make sure the change is shown the next time the user sees the permission.

Strongly Recommend: When you ask users for permissions, translate technical terms into more common ones. For example, instead of asking whether the MIDlet can "use a datagram receiver API," ask whether it can use airtime. Figure 15.5 shows a question from the MIDP Reference Implementation that uses ordinary instead of technical language.

15.6   Changing Permission Settings

MIDP implementors need to give users a way to edit the permission settings for MIDlet suites. As Figure 15.7 shows, the settings are usually most relevant for untrusted MIDlets but the security setting for the auto-invoke function group impacts trusted MIDlets as well. (See "Security for Push Functionality" on page 228 for more information.)

Settings for TicketLand:	Settings for TicketLand:	Settings for TicketLand:
Is it OK for TicketLand to interrupt another application to receive information? The interrupted application will exit.	Is it OK for TicketLand to send and receive information? This may result in charges to your bill.	Is it OK for TicketLand to directly connect to a computer in order to exchange information? This may require a special cable.
○ Yes, always. ⊙ Yes, but not when another application is running. ○ Ask me each time. ○ No. Don't interrupt.	○ Yes, always. ⊙ Ask me once per usage. ○ Ask me each time. ○ No. Don't use airtime.	○ Yes, always. ⊙ Ask me once per usage. ○ Ask me each time. ○ No. Don't connect.
Cancel Save	Cancel Save	Cancel Save

Figure 15.7 MIDP Reference Implementation's Settings User Interface

This section covers two approaches to giving users access to permission settings: accessing permission settings from the operating environment and accessing permission settings from inside a running MIDlet. (There are likely to be other alternatives too, depending on your device and operating environment.) In addition, this section covers an issue that has been difficult for users: understanding Oneshot and Session interaction levels.

MIDP Implementors

Strongly Recommend: Provide a way for users to change permission settings for MIDlet suites. (A MIDlet in a suite cannot have its own security settings.) Do usability studies to make sure the mechanism is straightforward and understandable.

15.6.1 Accessing Permission Settings From the Operating Environment

If a device already has a standard way to handle application settings from its operating environment, it should be possible to extend it to include security settings. Security settings would then be consistent with the operating environment of the device. For example, Figure 15.8 shows an operating environment, which has a standard menu, that includes an Application Settings command. Integrating the security settings into the existing application settings leverages the native user interface to make the security settings user interface more familiar to the user.

Figure 15.8 Access to Security Settings

MIDP Implementors

> *Consider*: Enable users to access permission settings from the operating environment if it is consistent with the behavior of your device, and you use native application-management functionality to manage MIDlet suites. (See Chapter 13 for information on application management.) If your device integrates MIDP and native applications, then going to the device settings may be more natural than looking for them elsewhere.

15.6.2 Accessing Permission Settings From Inside a MIDlet

If a device already has a standard way to handle application settings from within its applications, users will most likely also look for them within MIDlets. The MIDP implementation could enable the user to access security settings from within the running MIDlet by adding a command to the system menu, or whatever mechanism works for the device.

Giving users the ability to set security settings within a running MIDlet makes the task faster if they are already running the MIDlet. For example, there is no need for the user to exit the MIDlet to gain access to the settings user interface. However, if the user needs to change the settings for a MIDlet they are not running, this approach can be slower and more cumbersome.

MIDP Implementors

> *Consider*: Enable users to access permission settings from inside a MIDlet if it is consistent with the behavior of the device. If users expect to find these kinds of settings inside an application, they will most likely look for them inside a MIDlet too.

If you use put access to permission settings inside the MIDlet, you must take extra care to let the user know that security settings apply to the entire MIDlet suite. This will be easier if your device exposes users to the concept of a MIDlet suite (for example, if your device has users launch a MIDlet suite and then presents an intermediate screen of choices if the suite has more than one MIDlet, as described in "Launching and Exiting MIDlet Suites" on page 190). In this case, users will be better equipped to understand that a MIDlet is part of a "package" and that security settings affect the entire package.

However, if your device does not expose users to the concept of a MIDlet suite, you should let users know exactly which MIDlets would be affected by a change in the setting.

> *Consider*: When changing settings on MIDlet suites with multiple MIDlets, consider informing users that the settings apply to all MIDlets in the suite.

15.6.3 Oneshot and Session Permissions

Usability studies have shown that users have a difficult time understanding the oneshot and session interaction modes even when these terms are translated into something less technical.

Because oneshot must ask the user for permission every time a protected API is accessed, it can easily result in extremely annoying behavior in which the user is bombarded with multiple permission requests. In usability testing, users rarely understood the correlation between what they were doing on the screen and the prompts coming up, so it was difficult for them to figure out how to make them stop. When users did figure out Oneshot behavior, they, understandably, didn't like it.

The session interaction level was confusing because users had no concept of a session. Once again, they did not correlate what they did on their device when they started an application with the idea that a "session" had started. The term session is technical jargon.

One way to present these terms to users is to use phrases such as "Ask me every time." Figure 15.9 shows a user interface for setting permission levels.

Figure 15.9   Permission Settings User Interface

15.7   Security for Push Functionality

Auto-invoke functionality is the ability of a MIDlet to be launched in order to accept information that has been *pushed* to the device (sent to the device without the device initiating the connection) or in response to an alarm. (See Chapter 14 for information on auto-invoke functionality.)

Auto-invoke functionality is protected because it not only uses airtime, but it also has the ability to interrupt the user. A MIDlet that uses this functionality could interrupt a user at anytime, even when another MIDlet is running. Because of the interruption behavior, push applications require extra user-interface prompts and settings.

15.7.1   Prompts during Registration

A MIDlet that uses auto-invoke functionality must be registered with the MIDP implementation so that it can be launched in response to an incoming message. During installation, a MIDlet suite can register one or more of its MIDlets to use push functionality. In addition, a running MIDlet can register itself or another MIDlet in its suite to use the push or alarm functionality.

When a MIDlet suite tries to register during installation, MIDP asks the user for permission to put the application in the push registry, in addition to asking the user for permission to use airtime. The screens shown in Figure 15.10 demonstrate this sequence.

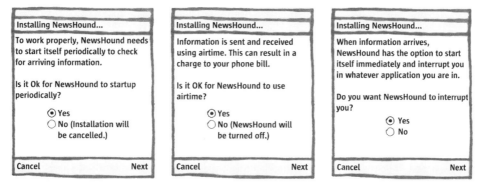

Figure 15.10 Screens during Installation of a Push-Enabled MIDlet Suite

When a running MIDlet tries to register to use the push or alarm functionality, similar screens will be shown to the user.

MIDP Implementors

Recommend: Streamline your push prompts so that the user realizes they are connected. Make the prompts feel like they are an integrated part of the installation.

15.7.2 Interruptions to Launch a MIDlet

When a successfully installed auto-invoke MIDlet receives a message, or reaches its alarm time, MIDP will try to start it so that it can act on that pushed data. When this happens, the user may be interrupted.

Settings for interruption behavior are critical. In usability studies, users generally wanted control over push services, such as news, so that they would not be interrupted when they were running another application. Even though they had signed up for a service that sent data, they wanted to be able to control when interruptions occurred. Figure 15.11 shows a screen asking the user whether it can interrupt.

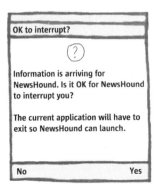

Figure 15.11 Interruption Alert

MIDP Implementors

 Recommend: Set a policy for interruptions on your device. For example, decide whether MIDlets can interrupt other running MIDlets, or whether the user can choose to be interrupted only when the device is idle. (See Chapter 14 for more information.)

If the user chooses a security setting that blocks push MIDlets from starting while another MIDlet is running, then start the push MIDlet as soon as the device is idle.

Remember that even trusted MIDlets that use push functionality should provide a user interface to control interruption behavior: Figure 15.12 shows a dialog box in which users can set the behavior of the MIDP Reference Implementation.

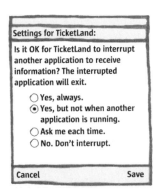

Figure 15.12 Settings for the Interruption Behavior of the Push Technology

CHAPTER 16

Advanced Topics

THIS chapter covers touch input, performance, and multithreading.

16.1   Touch Input

Devices have many different input methods, such as buttons, keyboards, and touch. This section provides guidelines for implementing and using touch input.

MIDP Implementors

> *Consider*: If a device has touch input, incorporate it into MIDP's high-level UI components so that users can interact with MIDlets in the same way that they interact with native applications. This follows the advice, "Make It Predictable" on page 9. For example, Figure 16.1 shows Sun's MIDP for Palm OS, which enables users to select an element of an exclusive-choice list by tapping it.

Figure 16.1   Exclusive-Choice List

MIDP Implementors, Continued

 Recommend: If a device has touch input, make it available to application developers for use on their canvas and game canvas screens.

Application Developers

Test whether a MIDP implementation offers touch input by calling the methods hasPointerEvents and hasPointerMotionEvents of the Canvas class. If a device has pointer events, you will be able to tell where a user tapped on the screen. If a device has pointer motion events, you will also be able to tell when a user drags a pointing device from one point on the screen to another.

> *Consider*: If touch input is available, incorporate it into your Canvas screens.

For example, most screens in SmartTicket are structured, high-level screens (such as implicit lists). On a PDA, users interact with these screens using touch input. If SmartTicket's canvas screen (shown in Figure 16.2) also supports touch input, users can interact with it in the same way that they interact with the other, structured screens. If the Canvas screen does not respond to touch input, it feels very different from the rest of the application; it feels awkward and unusable. In usability testing, users thought that the application was broken.

Figure 16.2 SmartTicket Canvas

16.1.1 Usability of Canvas and Game Canvas Screens

Application Developers

> *Consider*: Tailor the behavior of your Canvas and Game Canvas screens to the types of interaction devices support. A Canvas screen that can accept touch input should also accept game controls or phone keypad input (game controls are preferable to the phone keypad, as noted in Chapter 10). Incorporating the flexibility to use both touch and key input will enable the screens to behave predictably on the widest range of devices.

For example, the Push Puzzle game, shown in Figure 16.3, should accept game controls on all devices. It could add touch input, if a device has it available, so that users could tap on the screen to indicate the box's new location. It could add support for using the stylus to drag the box to its new location if a device also supports pointer motion events. The ability to use whatever input methods the device has available will give the application the ability to integrate well into the maximum number of devices.

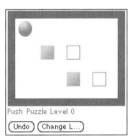

Figure 16.3 Push Puzzle Game

> *Consider*: Include a Help screen that explains how to operate your Canvas screen. The Help screen should explain how to use all types of input that the screen accepts. For example, Figure 16.4 shows a Help screen that explains how to use the game controls and a touch screen with the SmartTicket canvas.

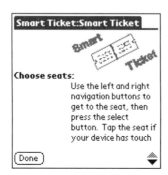

Figure 16.4   Help Screen That Explains How to Use a Canvas

Application Developers, Continued

> *Consider*: Test your touch-sensitive application with users on platforms that have and do not have touch input. This will ensure that your application is usable.

> *Consider*: If your MIDlet does not support touch input, notify consumers with product documentation and Help screens. Consumers with touch-input devices might be less frustrated by the difference in behavior if you tell them how to operate the application and they know what to expect.

16.1.2   Sizing Touch-Sensitive Components

Touch-sensitive components must be an appropriate size. If they are too small, users will have a difficult time tapping them accurately.

MIDP Implementors

> *Consider*: Determine the sizes of your touch-sensitive components, such as buttons, by examining successful native applications. For example, Figure 16.5 shows that the buttons used by a high-level component of a MIDP implementation are the same height and shape as those of a native application on the same device.

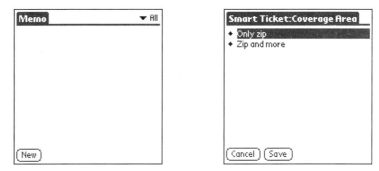

Figure 16.5 Buttons on a Native Application and a MIDP Application

Application Developers

Consider: Look to MIDP implementations on touch-sensitive devices as your model for the size of any touch-sensitive components you draw on a canvas.

Consider: Make output you draw to the Canvas screen scalable so that you can adapt it to the screen size of the device. (See "Accommodating Different Screen Sizes" on page 148 for more information.)

16.1.3 Interaction Styles

Both MIDP implementors and application developers should follow the same advice with respect to the way they expect users to interact with the touch screen. The advice in this section applies to both groups.

Application Developers and MIDP Implementors

Consider: Use a single tap interaction model. It is difficult to tap twice in the same spot with a stylus because of the human hand's natural jitter. Because it is error-prone, don't require double-tapping.

Consider: Typically, interactive components on a touch screen show a state change at a user's touch (stylus down) and execute when the touch releases (stylus up). The state change could be as simple as turning on the highlight. For example, Figure 16.6 shows the state change that takes place when the user touches an abstract command button on the Movie List screen of SmartTicket.

Figure 16.6   State Change When Abstract Command Is Touched

This model decreases user error because the highlight shows users what would happen if they released their touch at their current screen location. If users do not want to take the highlighted action, they can move their point of contact with the screen to a point outside the highlighted area before releasing. Components that follow this model are predictable, and easier to learn and use.

Application Developers and MIDP Implementors, Continued

> *Consider*: Make obvious targets active and touchable. For example, when using elements like check boxes or radio buttons, allow users to tap either on the text or the associated box or button. They expect both to operate the item or list element. Making these obvious targets selectable will make the MIDP implementation or the application's canvas screen less error-prone and more user friendly.

16.2   Performance

Performance depends on both MIDP implementors and application developers. Even if a user interface is well designed, if it runs slowly it will be unacceptable to users.

Different MIDP implementations can have different performance characteristics. Both hardware and software can cause the differences. As a result, a MIDlet could perform well on one device, but not on another.

MIDP Implementors

> *Consider*: Publish what developers should and should not do on your device. For example, let them know if your device has a special hardware-accelerated implementation of sprites.

Application developers can make educated guesses about how your device will perform, but if you provide the information, developers can do a better job more efficiently. For example, they could tailor the amount of network access done in their MIDlet for the type of network your device runs on. A GPRS network performs differently from a second-generation network in terms of network speed and latency.

Application Developers

> *Consider*: Adjust your MIDlet to the performance characteristics of a number of devices to provide a better user experience.

16.2.1 Measure Performance

In order to find out how long it takes to do a certain task, MIDP implementors and application developers can use *benchmarks*. Benchmarks are tests of the speed of certain actions or calculations on the device. On devices that run MIDP, benchmarks can measure performance of the LCDUI package, graphics, RMS, and networking.

Benchmarks can test two types of performance: raw and perceived. Typically MIDP implementors are more concerned with raw performance. For example, they would like to find and improve the speed of calculations in the virtual machine. Application developers are typically more concerned with perceived performance. For example, the first thing users sense is how quickly the MIDlet's first screen appears.

Application Developers and MIDP Implementors

Consider: Use benchmarks created for MIDP devices. For example, Caffeine Mark has a special version of their tests, called Embedded Caffeine Mark. In addition, the Embedded Microprocessor Benchmark Consortium (EEMBC) [26], which provides certified benchmarks for devices with embedded microprocessors, is working on a set for different areas of CLDC and MIDP. Benchmarks for the J2SE platform may not be suitable for MIDP.

Consider: Run benchmarks on a real device. Although you can start out using a simulator or emulator, the only way to get performance measurements you can trust is by using the device itself.

Application Developers

Consider: Create high-level benchmarks, if necessary, to test the speed of common tasks your MIDlet will perform. In addition, test any underlying tasks used by multiple higher-level functions, if those tasks are not covered by an existing benchmark. For example, if you are creating entertainment MIDlets, test the speed with which graphics are drawn. If you are creating business applications, test the speed of tasks such as opening connections.

Consider: Run lower-level benchmarks in addition to any that you write, because raw performance affects the duration of your higher-level tasks.

Benchmarks point out the strengths and weaknesses in performance in both the MIDP implementation and MIDlets. This information often reveals a trade-off between performance and user-interface style. Upcoming sections provide advice that can improve perceived performance without sacrificing your user interface.

16.2.2 Improving Perceived Performance

Improving perceived performance often means implementing the general advice, "Streamline Important Tasks for Efficiency" on page 10. Ensuring that the user needs to do the minimum amount of navigation and user interactions to accomplish frequent, important tasks helps them to get their tasks done more easily.

Following the general advice, "Provide Constant, Unobtrusive Feedback" on page 11, also improves perceived performance. The feedback could be with progress bars in forms or on alerts. (See Chapter 8 and Chapter 9 for information.)

Finally, keeping the user in control by following the general advice, "Make Everything Interruptible" on page 13, helps the user to feel that they are in control of the device. They will be more comfortable if they can stop a process that they feel is taking too long.

A specific area that is critical to perceived performance is startup time. Users expect applications on their devices to start quickly.

Application Developers

> *Consider*: If your MIDlet might have a long startup time, perform the long-running activities in a new thread and provide feedback while the MIDlet starts. The feedback could be a progress bar or a Splash screen. If users can see something happening, they will be less frustrated. This advice applies the principles from "Make It Responsive" on page 10.

Use the following list as a guide to running initialization in a new thread and providing feedback while the MIDlet starts:

- Do not put long-running initialization in the MIDlet constructor: you cannot show the user a screen until the `startApp` method returns.

- In the `startApp` method, create the Feedback screen and call the `setCurrent` method so that the system displays it when `startApp` returns. For example, you could create a Splash screen using a form with items that include a continuous-running gauge. (See Chapter 8 for more information.)

- In the `startApp` method, start a background thread to perform the long-running initialization so that the `startApp` method can return without waiting for the initialization to complete.

- Make the last action of the initialization thread a call that moves the display from the Feedback screen to the first screen of your application.

MIDP Implementors

Recommend: Publish whether your device preprocesses MIDlet suites during installation. Application developers writing MIDlets for devices that preprocess MIDlets have fewer concerns about startup times.

Recommend: Publish what happens during a long startup or shutdown. For example, publish whether you provide an animated Startup screen.

16.2.3 Improving Perceived Graphics Performance

Smooth graphics are important to perceived performance. Users should not see screen flickering due to screen redrawing, nor should they be able to watch the screen redraw. If this is an issue, follow the advice in "Avoiding Flicker" on page 150.

16.2.4 Profiling

If you still have perceived performance problems after you have followed the advice in the previous sections, use a profiler to see where the time is being spent. You can try a profiler that runs in a PC environment, but the results are less reliable than using a profiler while running on a real device.

With the information from the profiler, you can improve the areas of the code that are taking too much time. Many of the hints that have been published for improving a J2SE platform application also apply to a MIDP application. For example, *Effective Java™ Programming Language Guide (Java Series)* [15] has the advice, "Know and Use the Libraries." This applies to J2ME applications too. For example, do not use a canvas to create your own high-level components. Use the components from the LCDUI package. Using the high-level components instead of creating your own will improve the package size and runtime memory usage of your MIDlet.

16.2.5 Improving Perceived Performance from RMS

Profiling may show that using the record management system (RMS) is a performance issue. To maintain the integrity of a MIDlet's data, the MIDP implementation has to save data in persistent storage, and in many devices, this means the device has to write to flash memory. Flash memory can be slower than other types of memory.

Application Developers

Consider: Minimize your read and write operations if RMS is a bottleneck. When you do need to use RMS, provide feedback during the saving process.

Consider: Write to RMS when your application is starting up and shutting down. While your application is running and your user interface is visible, store data in runtime objects. (Make sure you can do this with minimal object overhead so that runtime memory use does not become an issue.)

16.3 Multithreading

Multiple threads are available within a Java virtual machine. Both the MIDP implementor and the application developer need to use these threads safely. Using threads safely means that shared data never becomes corrupted, even in the presence of concurrent access, and that the system is live (threads do not deadlock).

16.3.1 Thread Safety

The *Java™ Tutorial: A Short Course on the Basics (Third Edition)* [16], has information on how to properly protect shared information in the Java programming language. This section provides some MIDP-specific suggestions and requirements.

Applications must be allowed to define and implement their own locking policies for their own data structures, without any restrictions from LCDUI beyond those imposed by the *MIDP 2.0 Specification* [19]. Applications should be free to use locks even on LCDUI objects, and to create subclasses of LCDUI classes without violating any safety guarantees.

MIDP Implementors

Strongly Recommend: Ensure that calls into LCDUI from any thread or class outside the package leave LCDUI in a valid and consistent state. For example, it should not be possible for an application's threads to concurrently update a list, and to have some changes appear but not others. If one thread adds two elements to a list, while another changes two existing elements, the list should, after running the calls, have the two updated elements and the two new elements.

Application Developers

If your MIDlet is multithreaded, define and use a locking policy in your application that protects its shared data without deadlocking.

Strongly Recommend: Build into your locking policy the *MIDP 2.0 Specification* requirement regarding the serviceRepaints method of the Canvas class. That requirement states that if your application calls the serviceRepaints method, it does so without holding any lock that your implementation of the paint method might acquire. If you violate this prohibition, deadlock could result.

16.3.2 Responsiveness

In addition to keeping their applications deadlock free and safe, application developers must also be concerned about responsiveness. (See "Make It Responsive" on page 10 for information.) Specifically, *callbacks* need to be responsive, and they can be most responsive when multiple threads are used appropriately.

A callback is a method that an application developer writes and a device calls to perform a task at appropriate times. A MIDP implementation informs a MIDlet about user actions, such as selecting an abstract command, through callbacks, such as the commandAction method.

Strongly Recommend: Do not perform any task in a callback that has the potential to take a long time, such as network operations. Instead, arrange for the work to be done in another thread. (See *Networking, User Experience, and Threads* [27] and *Making HTTP Connections Using Background Threads* [28] for information.)

Bibliography

Consumer Design Publications

[1]   Bergman, Eric, ed. *Information Appliances and Beyond: Interaction Design for Consumer Products*, Morgan Kaufmann Publishers, San Francisco, 2000. ISBN: 1-55860600-9

[2]   Weiss, Scott. *Handheld Usability,* John Wiley & Sons, Ltd, West Sussex, England, 2002. ISBN: 0-470-84446-9

General Design Publications

[3]   Baecker, Ronald M., William Buxton, and Jonathan Grudin, eds. *Readings in Human-Computer Interaction: Toward the Year 2000*, 2nd ed. Morgan Kaufmann, San Francisco, 1995. ISBN: 0-934613-24-9

[4]   Green, William S., and Patrick W. Jordan. *Pleasure With Products: Beyond Usability*, Taylor & Francis, 2001. ISBN: 0-41523704-1

[5]   Isaacs, Ellen, and Alan Walendowski. *Designing from Both Sides of the Screen: How Designers and Engineers Can Collaborate to Build Cooperative Technology*, New Riders, Indianapolis, 2002. ISBN: 0-67232151-3

[6]   Jenson, Scott. *The Simplicity Shift: Innovative Design Tactics in a Corporate World*, Cambridge University Press, Cambridge, England, 2002. ISBN: 0-521-52749-X

[7]   Johnson, Jeff. GUI Bloopers: *Don'ts and Do's for Software Developers and Web Designers*, Morgan Kaufmann, San Francisco, 2000. ISBN: 1-55860-582-7

[8]   Laurel, Brenda, ed. *Art of Human-Computer Interface Design*, Addison-Wesley, Palo Alto, CA, 1990. ISBN: 0-201-51797-3

[9]   Mullet, Kevin, and Darrell Sano. *Designing Visual Interfaces: Communication Oriented Techniques*, Prentice Hall, Upper Saddle River, New Jersey, 1994. ISBN: 0-13-303389-9

[10]   Nielsen, Jakob. *Usability Engineering*, Academic Press, Boston, 1993. ISBN: 0-12-518405-0

[11]   Norman, Donald A. *The Design of Everyday Things*, Doubleday, New York, 1990. ISBN: 0465067107

[12]   Shneiderman, Ben. *Designing the User Interface: Strategies for Effective Human-Computer Interaction, Third Edition*, Addison-Wesley, Reading, MA 1997. ISBN: 0201694972

[13]   Tognazzini, Bruce. *Tog on Software Design*, Addison-Wesley, Palo Alto, CA, 1995. ISBN 0-201-60842-1

[14]   Tufte, Edward R. *The Visual Display of Quantitative Information*, Graphics Press, Cheshire, CT, 1992. ISBN 0-9613921-0-X

MIDP Programming Publications

[15]   Bloch, Joshua. *Effective Java™ Programming Language Guide*, Addison-Wesley, Boston, 2001. ISBN: 0201310058.
       <http://java.sun.com/docs/books/effective/>

[16]   Campione, Mary, Kathy Walrath, and Alison Huml. *The Java™ Tutorial: A Short Course on the Basics, Third Edition*, Addison-Wesley, Boston, 2003. ISBN: 0201703939.
       <http://java.sun.com/docs/books/tutorial/index.html>

[17]   Riggs, Roger, Antero Taivalsaari, and Mark VandenBrink. *Programming Wireless Devices with the Java™ 2 Platform, Micro Edition, Second Edition,* Addison-Wesley, Boston, 2003. ISBN: 0321197984.
`<http://java.sun.com/docs/books/j2mewireless/index.html>`

[18]   Java 2 Platform Micro Edition, Wireless Toolkit.
`<http://java.sun.com/products/j2metoolkit/>`

[19]   Java Specification Requests (JSRs) for the J2ME Platform.
`<http://jcp.org/jsr/tech/j2me.jsp>`

[20]   Mobile Information Device Profile (MIDP) Reference Implementation.
`<http://java.sun.com/products/midp/>`

[21]   MIDP for Palm OS.
`<http://java.sun.com/products/midp4palm/>`

[22]   BluePrints: Guidelines, Patterns and Code (including a version of the SmartTicket example used throughout this book).
`<http://java.sun.com/blueprints/>`

[23]   Java 2 Platform Micro Edition (J2ME).
`<http://wireless.java.sun.com/j2me/>`

Web Publications

[24]   *PNG (Portable Network Graphics) Specification,* Version 1.0, October 1996.
`<http://www.w3.org/TR/REC-png.html>`

[25]   *PNG (Portable Network Graphics) Specification,* Version 1.0, RFC 2083, March 1997.
`<http://www.ietf.org/rfc/rfc2083.txt>`

[26]   Embedded Microprocessor Benchmark Consortium.
`<http://www.eembc.org>`

[27]   Knudson, Jonathan. *Networking, User Experience, and Threads*, January 2002.
<http://wireless.java.sun.com/midp/articles/threading/>

[28]   Giguere, Eric. *Making HTTP Connections Using Background Threads*, December 2000.
<http://wireless.java.sun.com/midp/ttips/httpthrds/>

Index

The Java™ Series

ISBN 0-201-63456-2

ISBN 0-201-70433-1

ISBN 0-201-31005-8

ISBN 0-201-79168-4

ISBN 0-201-70393-9

ISBN 0-201-48558-3

ISBN 0-201-74622-0

ISBN 0-201-75280-8

ISBN 0-201-76810-0

ISBN 0-201-31002-3

ISBN 0-201-31003-1

ISBN 0-201-48552-4

ISBN 0-201-71102-8

ISBN 0-201-70329-7

ISBN 0-201-30955-6

ISBN 0-201-31008-2

ISBN 0-201-78472-6

ISBN 0-201-78791-1

ISBN 0-201-31009-0

ISBN 0-201-70502-8

ISBN 0-201-32577-2

ISBN 0-201-43294-3

ISBN 0-201-91466-2

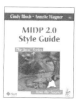
ISBN 0-321-19801-8

ISBN 0-201-74627-1

ISBN 0-201-70456-0

ISBN 0-201-77580-8

ISBN 0-201-78790-3

ISBN 0-201-71041-2

ISBN 0-201-77582-4

ISBN 0-201-43321-4

ISBN 0-201-43328-1

ISBN 0-201-70969-4

ISBN 0-321-17384-8

Visit http://www.awprofessional.com/javaseries for more information on these titles.

Register Your Book

at www.awprofessional.com/register

You may be eligible to receive:

- Advance notice of forthcoming editions of the book
- Related book recommendations
- Chapter excerpts and supplements of forthcoming titles
- Information about special contests and promotions throughout the year
- Notices and reminders about author appearances, tradeshows, and online chats with special guests

Contact us

If you are interested in writing a book or reviewing manuscripts prior to publication, please write to us at:

Editorial Department
Addison-Wesley Professional
75 Arlington Street, Suite 300
Boston, MA 02116 USA
Email: AWPro@aw.com

Addison-Wesley

Visit us on the Web: http://www.awprofessional.com